MODERNITY'S PRETENSES

MODERNITY'S PRETENSES

Making Reality Fit Reason from *Candide* to the Gulag

KARLIS RACEVSKIS

STATE UNIVERSITY OF NEW YORK PRESS

Published by
State University of New York Press, Albany

For information, address State University of New York Press,
State University Plaza, Albany, NY, 12246

Production by Cathleen Collins
Marketing by Anne Valentine

Library of Congress Cataloging-in-Publication Data

Racevskis, Karlis.
    Modernity's pretenses : making reality fit reason from Candide to
the gulag / Karlis Racevskis.
        p.   cm. — (SUNY series in postmodern culture)
    Includes bibliographical references and index.
    ISBN 0-7914-3953-4 (alk. paper). — ISBN 0-7914-3954-2 (pbk. :
alk. paper)
    1. Rationalism—Controversial literature. 2. Reason—History.
3. Postmodernism. I. Title. II. Series.
B833.R22 1998
149'.7—dc21   97-43903
                                                                              CIP

10 9 8 7 6 5 4 3 2 1

For Maija

Contents

Preface

The metaphor of pretense that serves as the central theme for my project is to be understood in terms of the original, Latin sense of the verb *praetendere*, which refers to the action of drawing a curtain in front of a stage or a scene. I take it to sum up a procedure that is characteristic of attempts at capturing the meaning or the truth of "reality." In my previous book, *Postmodernism and the Search for Enlightenment* (Virginia, 1993), I argued that a critique of such attempts constitutes a major theme of structuralist and poststructuralist criticism. In this regard, the notion of pretense can also be understood as a principle of noncorrespondence and it has been used to illustrate the ways in which Western society has developed a pattern of creating images and discourses about itself that actually serve to cover up or veil other processes essential to its functioning. The present book elaborates on this line of thinking and studies in greater detail several concrete instances of pretending. The purpose is to consider the production of abstract systems of rationalizing as a basic strategy marking the installation and maintenance of the historicocultural period known as modernity.

The modernist outlook was based on the idea of a generally stable relationship between self and reality, subject and object. The self was conceived as an autonomous, consciousness fully endowed with the capacity to represent and understand the objects, phenomena, and events making up its life experience. The essential purpose of this active and responsible self was to achieve a fundamental knowledge and to establish truths about reality. When properly applied, this knowledge was deemed to possess the capacity for modifying and transforming reality, especially the socioeconomic kind, and thus for bringing about progress in human affairs. The principle that guaranteed the viability as well as the success of this process of the gradual enlightenment of humanity and the amelioration of its condition was reason—the mysterious yet efficacious motive for justifying comprehension as well as action, the undefinable quality that stood for the very essence of humanity.

It has become obvious that modernity's promise of control and progress was premature, to say the least. What stands out today, are glaring discrepancies between modernity's claims and the effects achieved. As knowledge has increased and information proliferated, our ignorance about the world, about ourselves, has expanded proportionally. Instead of achieving control over our natural and human environment, it seems we are evermore vulnerable to the force of the intangible, the unexpected, and the contingent. Just as it has been impossible to tame nature, the attempt to impose control and order in the name of principles considered eternal and absolute appears as frustrating as ever. The single-minded reliance on Reason has increasingly brought out the mighty effect of Unreason in human affairs. Aspects of our civilization that seemed amenable to the influence of reason do not seem to make sense anymore. Instead of progress, we see an unsettling increase in the dangers that the process of an uncontrollable and unpredictable change has brought about. The menace of ecological, nuclear, and other disasters, the threat of civil strife and global disorder, the uncontrollable rise in domestic violence and international terrorism, all have become the distinctive features of the current stage in our civilization.

It is in this sense that the postmodern condition can be seen in terms of a disaffection, a disillusionment stemming from the evident discrepancy between a well-intentioned and ambitious civilizing purpose and the contradictory results that have been achieved. It seems indeed, to use Zygmunt Bauman's apt expression, that "postmodernity is modernity coming to terms with its own impossibility." Everything indicates that we have outgrown our capacity for understanding ourselves and our world according to the terms set by modernity. Our experience now overwhelms our ability to make sense according to the rational, ethical, and aesthetic standards at our disposal.

History, according to one definition, is nothing more than the story of humanity's growing self-awareness. There are evidently moments in the evolution of humankind when this questioning becomes particularly intense and absorbing, when the question of the present and its meaning imposes itself with a particular urgency. The postmodern awareness of present dilemmas and dis-appointments is very likely a symptom of such a historical juncture. It can be seen as a response to the currently perceived need to explore the significance of the present moment in the evolution of our civilization, to search out manifestations of the trends and transformations taking place in the present configuration of cultural, social, political, and economic forces.

What present-day critiques of our cultural imaginary provide most notably is an awareness of the irreducible complexity of our world; they also bring out the reasons why the process of making sense of the world and of creating norms by which to live is more demanding than modernity imagined. A postmodern critical perspective makes us understand that, on the one hand, this sense and these norms are not available to us preformed, that they have not been inscribed from the beginning of time in a book of eternal and universal verities. On the other hand, once they are brought down to earth, the values and meanings that inform our lives become our responsibility once more: we now know that, if they are to be, these norms and this sense need to be reaffirmed, reformulated, or created anew through a never-ending process of debate and negotiations. It is toward the expansion and promotion of this process that the present work hopes to contribute.

Two of the chapters in this book reproduce material that has already appeared in print. Chapter 3 was first published as "The Postmodern Outlook for Hermeneutics," *Diacritics* 24.1 (1994): 78–90. Chapter 6 incorporates three articles: "Voices from the Gulag: A Review Essay," *Journal of Baltic Studies* 24.3 (1993): 299–306; "The Literary Experience of the Gulag: Loss and Recovery of Identity," *Germano-Slavica* 8.2 (1994): 17–22; and "Finding Our Roots in Exile: Folklore versus the Humanities," *World Literature Today* 61.1 (1987): 9–12. My concluding remarks on the postcolonial situation are exerpted from a review article published in *Research in African Literatures* 29.2 (1998): 214–18.

Introduction

The desire to control reality has clearly been one of the driving motives behind the Western project of civilization since the days of Bacon and Descartes. It has manifested itself as an urge to impose order on the profusion of signs speaking for the world and has materialized as an explanatory paradigm that pretends to translate chaos into a manageable representation. Underlying this purpose was a supreme confidence in the human capacity to know and to apply knowledge. Max Oelschlager gives a particularly cogent explanation of the hubris inherent in Western culture:

> Painting with a broad brush, it is permissible to say that prior to the twentieth century most modern people, including intellectuals, believed that a sure and certain knowledge of the world was theoretically possible, if not actualized in practice. So-called modernists typically believe that human reason—epitomized by modern science—is supreme, that it exists without limits, as it were, that the whole world lies open to disclosure by human intelligence.[1]

While this attitude has become an ingrained habit of the modern mind, it has also served to bring out an increasingly glaring discrepancy between the boast and the results achieved. As a result, certain forms of discourse elaborated by modernity call attention to themselves for the very hollowness of the claims they have attempted to sustain.

Doubtless, humans have always attempted to make sense of the chaos around them. What makes modernity stand out, however, is a propensity for considering its pretenses real. This tendency has become second nature to it and could be considered one of its defining characteristics. The reality thus created is doubly convenient. It has been scaled down to human size—which is to say that it is made to fit whatever model of humanity a given society valorizes at any given historical juncture. And it also helps forget and hide whatever may be operating behind the pretense: it is a reality made to order for those who derive comfort or profit from the subterfuge. According to Zygmunt Bauman, this duplicity is the telling characteristic of social existence in the modern age:

> We can say that existence is modern in as far as it is effected and sustained by *design, manipulation, management, engineering*. The existence is modern in as far as it is administered by resourceful (that is, possessing knowledge, skill and technology), sovereign agencies. Agencies are sovereign in as far as they claim and successfully defend the right to manage and administer existence: the right to define order and, by implication, lay aside chaos, as that left-over that escapes the definition.[2]

For D. H. Lawrence, the obsession with covering up chaos is what distinguishes us from animals. We cannot live in chaos, according to Lawrence, but:

> The animals can. To the animal all is chaos, only there are a few recurring motions and aspects within the surge. And the animal is content. But man is not. Man must wrap himself in a vision, make a house of apparent form and stability, fixity. In his terror of chaos he begins by putting up an umbrella between himself and the everlasting whirl. Then he paints the underside of his umbrella. Bequeathed to his descendants, the umbrella becomes a dome, a vault, and men at last begin to feel that something is wrong.[3]

This frantic activity to devise a cover for chaos is futile in the long run because the pretense will eventually prove unsatisfactory and someone will inevitably challenge it. For D. H. Lawrence, it is the poet who is most likely to assume this responsibility: "Then comes a poet, enemy of convention, and makes a slit in the umbrella; and lo! the glimpse of chaos is a vision, a window to the sun. But after a while, getting used to the vision, and not liking the genuine draught from chaos, commonplace man daubs a simulacrum of the window that opens on to chaos, and patches the umbrella with the painted patch of the simulacrum."[4] The poet's task of revealing chaos is therefore endless, while the work of patching goes on relentlessly. In the long run, the umbrella solidifies and becomes enormous. The patchwork of simulacra hardens to the point where it becomes impossible to make new slits and, as a result, "the umbrella is absolute. And so the yearning for chaos becomes a nostalgia. And this will go on till some terrific wind blows the umbrella to ribbons, and much of mankind to oblivion. The rest will shiver in the midst of chaos."[5]

In ancient Greek, *apokalypsos* stood for tearing away a veil or a covering. In this sense, postmodernism can be seen as the apocalypse of modernity—although the tearing away of pretenses has been gradual rather than violent: the process has been going on for over a century and is still very much in progress. It is a process already identified by Nietzsche, who was acutely aware of the laughable fragility of all the discursive strategies devised for coping with chaos in a hostile universe:

> Not only did he teach the truth that we have to live without truth, he taught that we have to live within a noisy and meaningless silence. What is language? Consider the hostility of the universe. That hostility is like a fierce sun burning down upon us. Language is the parasol we hold above our heads to protect ourselves. Oh, we say, we are safe here. Nothing can harm us because we have our parasol of little words![6]

The world humanity has created for itself is itself becoming unmanageable and therefore causing us to doubt the explanations and justifications carefully constructed over the past two or three centuries. These discourses can no longer claim to represent or control reality for us because, as Jean-Luc Nancy observes, the reality of these times is to be found in the faults opened up by the failure of meaning, the failure of humanism and civilization to make sense: it is a reality to be found "in extermination, in exploitation, in hunger, in technique, in art, in literature, in philosophy."[7] Our world, argues Nancy, no longer makes sense, no longer knows what to make of itself, and has been reduced to an enumeration: "It is an endless list—and in fact, everything is happening as if our only option were but to draw up this list, in an accounting that allows for no bottom line. It is a litany—that is, a prayer, but of pure suffering, of pure loss and bewilderment, a wailing that is heard daily from the mouths of the millions of refugees, of the deported, the besieged, the mutilated, the starved, the raped, the cut off, the excluded, the exiled, and the expulsed."[8] The pretense of idealist and humanist discourses not only fails to provide an explanation for the disarray of the world but could be considered to some degree responsible for this condition since, as Foucault and other critics have shown, the deployment of discourses of virtue and values has greatly contributed to occlude the workings of power and strategies of domination and it is often the blindness and complicity of a well-meaning and moralizing piety "that have given free reign to everything that has given our century's humanity reason to despair of itself."[9]

The philosophical, religious, artistic, scientific, resources that gave meaning to humanity are today exhausted:

> Christianity and empiricism have led us to ourselves, they have been our destiny, as has democracy, and axiomatics, and the critique of reason, and the rights of man, and art for art's sake, and total man, etc. But in the end, the system and the history of signification wind up signifying their own annulment, turning around on themselves to reveal nothing more than the infinite distancing from the meaning that was meant, immobile and inaccessible, or endlessly fleeing: quietly becoming, as if under our very eyes, meaningless.[10]

This is to say that the meaning of our existence can no longer be referred to the metaphysical alibis of modernity and that "we find ourselves exposed once more to ourselves, once more to one another, and to our language, and to our world. Once more, *our* existence demands its sense and its rights. We can no longer allow ourselves to be presented with respect to the Heavens, to an Idea, or History, nor, in general, with respect to signification. We must exist in the sense that we are."[11] We no longer *have* meaning, because we *are* ourselves this meaning, Nancy tells us: "Being does not *have* meaning, but being itself, the phenomenon of being, is meaning, which is, in turn, its own circulation—and *we* are this circulation."[12] In light of this new "exigency of meaning," the fundamental pattern of dualisms that structure modern thinking such as the opposites of subject and object, mind and world, spirit and matter dissolve. The relationship between them is no longer a given.

Modernity, as Gordon Globus points out, "relies on representations of the world—mental and neural re-presentations that mediate between us and the world." Postmodernists no longer claim to be able to represent the world; and in this regard, explains Globus, "postmodernists are staunch realists. The world is there before us, just as we think it is. We do not know reality, according to postmodernism, by means of any representations of that reality. We know reality directly and immediately; there is nothing that gets between us and the reality we always already find ourselves in."[13] Such a view produces a dramatic reversal in the position of the subject, displacing it from the autonomous and authoritative position Bacon and Descartes had granted it to a dependent and decentered one. We have, in effect, "lost our selves," which are, as Globus puts it, "the selves we thought were primary and autonomous over against the independent world."[14] The duality of self and world turns out to have been derivative, it is a construct we have naturalized by turning its components into elemental wholes; as a consequence, we have lost the capacity to see that "the world *in its apparent outthereness* is a brain achievement. *The world that we always already find ourselves thrown in continually settles out of a spontaneous eruption.*"[15]

The idea that we are independent entities endowed with the capacity to observe and assimilate the world by filtering what we observe for the purpose of constituting knowledge that will enable us to oversee, manage, even control reality is basically misguided because it takes the process mediating between subject and object to be largely transparent. The merging of subject and object brings about a corresponding reorientation in our thinking by making the question of the relationship between the two the most pressing issue. It is the experience of subject and object and the representation of the experience that become the critical issues. What gets rejected, as a result, are the two concepts of Reason and Reality, since it was their seemingly indissoluble alliance that allowed for the elision of an area that now seems so crucial—which is the process mediating and/or constituting the perception of reality.

According to Foucault, one of the characteristics of the modern age is precisely the effort to escape the influence of Hegel, the philosopher who helped put in place the combined authority of these two abstractions.[16] In a like manner, Ernst Cassirer warns us that "we can give ourselves over today less than ever before to that optimism which Hegel's famous words express, 'what is rational is real; what is real is rational.'"[17] Implied in Cassirer's admonition is the suggestion that the pretense of appropriating reality through reason translates into a failure to examine what this telescoping of reason into reality allowed to cover up. In the first place, the cover-up amounts to a scandal that taints philosophy and "the failure of western philosophy to justify its own presumption of rationality is not unlike a family scandal, which imposes a certain discipline, if not a repressive silencing, lest the whole structure fall apart at the seams."[18] The cover-up also distorts and impoverishes our knowledge of ourselves and the world, as Todd May explains:"The philosophical and political focus upon a constitutive subjectivity has had as one of its results the neglect of the constitutive power of social practices. As long as people are perceived as largely self-constituting, the ways the social practices in which they are immersed not only limit but also produce that constitution is either ignored or relegated to a secondary status."[19] The stubbornness with which the West has clung to what Murray Code calls its "myths of reason" suggests indeed an obsession that verges on the pathological. Noting that a "desire for control is an excellent source of anxiety," Code wonders, "could it be that a fascination with logical methods and standards is a sign of a neurotic anxiety elicited by ambiguity and vagueness?"[20]

Modernity's reticence to question its own pretenses even in the face of growing evidence of the hollowness of its claims can be attributed to a strategy of self-preservation, argues Bauman: "For most of its history, modernity lived in and through self-deception. Concealment of its own parochiality, conviction that whatever is not universal in its particularity is but not-yet-universal, that the project of universality may be incomplete, but remains most definitely on, was the core of that self-deception. It was perhaps thanks to that self-deception that modernity could deliver both the wondrous and the gruesome things that it did."[21] The self-deception thus brought to the fore precisely what it had set out to exorcise—the fear of chaos. Ironically, by pretending that everything was under control, it unleashed the forces of chaos in their most murderous manifestations. Reason gave free reign to unreason by stubbornly clinging to a self-deluding sense of importance that kept it from seeing that it no longer had any hold on reality:

> The most extreme and well documented cases of global "social engineering" in modern history (those presided

over by Hitler and Stalin), all their attendant atrocities notwithstanding, were neither outbursts of barbarism not yet fully extinguished by the new rational order of civilization, nor the price paid for utopias alien to the spirit of modernity. On the contrary, they were legitimate offspring of the modern spirit, of that urge to assist and speed up the progress of mankind toward perfection that was throughout the most prominent hallmark of the modern age.[22]

The divorce of Reason from Reality was bound to bring about Reason's downfall since it became clear that each Reality requires the reason or reasons that suit its particular needs and circumstances. The Reason that achieved preeminence in the eighteenth century was the one that proved useful in combatting the ignorance and superstition of this particular age. As soon as these obstacles to progress became obsolete, Reason was no longer anchored to a concrete project. Consequently, it was turned into an abstract notion that could serve purposes of all sorts. It became the new political, cultural, and social regime with all the prerogatives and transcendent guarantees enjoyed by the old one: "Reason possesses, as did the monarchy, a perfectly constructed, perfectly integrated, perfectly self-justifying system."[23] Because Reason was self-sufficient, it could easily be used for the basest of purposes in the name of the highest values; it is a paradox that Schopenhauer found particularly intriguing: "A man can go to work rationally and thus thoughtfully, deliberately, consistently, systematically, and methodically, and yet act upon the most selfish, unjust, and even iniquitous maxims. . . . Reasonable and vicious are quite consistent with each other, and in fact, only through their union are great and far-reaching crimes possible."[24] Schopenhauer was thus bringing into question a connection that has been one of modernity's founding principles—the seemingly unbreakable bond between rationality and virtue.

The principal appeal of Reason thus appears to have resided in its capacity for providing reassuring answers by simplifying an otherwise unmanageable reality. This simplification is the sustaining theme of a tactic which, since the time of Descartes, has served to establish absolute certainty. As Susan Bordo explains, however, it is a tactic that can also be seen as a response to anxiety: "When the universe becomes unmanageable, human beings become absolutists. We create a world without ambiguity in order to escape, as Dewey puts it, 'from the vicissitudes of experience,' to impose order on what is experienced as without organic order of its own."[25]

For postmodernists, the comforts of such apodictic assertions as "what is rational is real and what is real is rational" are no longer available. At most, the experience of "reality" can be grasped through the distortions and filtering of accumulated conscious and unconscious experiences. "Every would-be knower approaches the world from within a complex web of symbolizations," notes Code; we therefore need to understand that "all talk about reality is really second hand talk about symbolizations."[26] Our mental habits are so deeply ingrained and have been assimilated so thoroughly that they have become a part of our very selves. As a result, we are not even aware of the process that makes possible our impression of "knowing" reality. Indeed, it makes no sense to even talk of "reality" since the talking is itself always/already a part of the reality it addresses. Thus, when we really think about it, "what reality is 'in itself' is unsayable" and any attempt to pose a question about the nature of reality is incoherent because "the very attempt to answer it already violates the conditions being excluded by the question, namely to say what 'things-in-themselves' are without using language."[27] Similarly, any talk of a world "out there" is self-contradictory because such a world is "but a self-referential system that 'talks about itself.' It 'thematises' itself through the epistemic activity of certain cognitive agents. There is no reality *independently* of such epistemic activity." Nevertheless, we must also recognize that we are inevitably led to posit such a reality and that "the 'naturalistic' conception of reality is deeply ingrained in our ordinary modes of thinking."[28] We must therefore keep in mind that "the world is not just a 'totality of objects,' or naturalistically conceived events, but is rather an arrangement whereby such objects, events, etc. present themselves as ontological existents to cognitive agents under certain concrete historical conditions."[29]

In short, we need to be constantly aware that "we confer intelligibility upon our experience of the world."[30] It is an awareness, moreover, which helps us discover that there are concepts that function mainly to elide or cover up this process of making things intelligible: they are the obstacles to understanding that, for Code, "deserve . . . to be called myths of reason, for they appear to be so deeply entrenched in common modes of thought as to be almost invisible."[31] Some of the most inconspicuous habits are simply due to the nature of the languages we use, to syntactical patterns that make subject-object relations, for example, appear inherently natural. Moreover, the use of language inculcates in the user the ineradicable belief "that whatever can be named must in some sense *be*."[32]

It is clear, at the same time, that symbolizing constitutes a profoundly human activity—we are symbolizing organisms and, as such, we are constantly engaged in sorting out and interpreting the profusion of signals that make up the world we are immersed in. At the most basic level, as biological organisms, we exist in an environment that is the real: "The real, one can say, is that which presents data to potential interpreters, and these presentations, depending on the kind of creatures involved, give rise to various representations."[33] Moreover, the conscious and rational part of our selves is only one aspect of this involvement with the presentations of our environment. Code reminds us that "science teaches us, for one thing, that we are an integral part of nature, completely immersed as organisms in a variety of experiences that relentlessly remind us that reality involves a host of types of response."[34] In this regard, the term *to perceive* is misleading and provides a good example of what Code calls myths of Reason. Owen Barfield has shown, for example, that the term to perceive leads us to confuse percept with its cause since "I do not hear undulating molecules of air . . . I do not touch a moving system of waves." Furthermore,

> I do not perceive any *thing* with my sense organs alone, but with a great part of my whole human being. Thus, I may say, loosely, that I "hear a thrush singing." But in strict truth all that I ever merely "hear"—all that I ever hear simply by virtue of having ears—is *sound*. When I "hear a thrush singing," I am hearing, not with my ears alone, but with all sorts of other things like mental habits, memory, imagination, feeling and (to the extent at least that the act of attention involves it) will.[35]

It is the sum of all these elements constituting a response to stimuli that makes up subjectivity. It is a subjectivity that is "implicit in every act of representing insofar as such acts involve an element of interpretation."[36] Perception resonates with other real or imagined experiences that a perceiving consciousness brings with it in its apprehension of the real; we therefore have to understand perception "as involving not only a relatively stable and definite world made up of readily available commonsense objects but also a complex tangle of hypothetical objects that are only more or less amenable to confirmation by sense experience."[37] One last difficulty standing in the way of our understanding of what is involved in our encounter with the real is the step leading from matter to mind, the process that transforms nerve impulses into conscious or subconscious thought. It is likely to remain forever a mystery as there is "reason to doubt that there are any logico-linguistic, let alone scientific means to analyze the processes that convert presentation into representation."[38]

Perception is therefore an impure and unfathomable operation. It carries with it motivations of which we are not aware; it is informed by memories and guided by anticipation. The materials available for representing are thus always already subject to an undisclosed and undefinable process of selection and valorization. What such a perspective on perception enables is an inversion of commonsensical assumptions about the nature of thought and its relation to perception. According to a common assumption, "the 'public' world (which is what we have in common with others) consists entirely of what we *perceive* and the private world of each one consists of what he *thinks* . . . the exact opposite is the case. It is the thought content which we share with others, while our percepts (so far as they are undetermined by *any* element of thought are private to ourselves."[39] Our manner of representing reality has to rely on commonly shared, acquired linguistic systems and conceptual schemes; unreflected perception is the individual organisms reaction to and interaction with its environment.

The idea of a systematic, logical, and controlled approach to reality that would result in an exact knowledge of this reality turns out to be one more pretense, therefore. Indeed, it is an idea that seems preposterous today: "Why should anyone expect to find chains of cause and effect in nature that are analogous to rigid logical chains of reasoning?" asks Code.[40] In the final account, the best we can say about representation is that it is a metaphor for something not amenable to Reason. It is not Reason that puts us in touch with reality but rather its opposites—instinct, emotion, and imagination. It is the conclusion of the English philosopher Alfred North Whitehead who was convinced that "creative imaginations informed by aesthetic feelings are at the bottom of successful connections between human knowers and reality."[41] The proof for this is to be found in all great works of literary, visual, and musical art since "the activity of symbolizing covers a much wider and richer field of sentience than that covered by words."[42]

As a device for representing reality, language also turns out to be highly inadequate and it almost goes without saying today that "words cannot precisely map all the wealth of the facts which they describe."[43] Yet language has the symbolic capacity to evoke the depth and complexity of reality and it is this symbolic potential that allows literature to transcend the limits of time and locale. Roland Barthes reminds us, for example, that "whatever societies may think or decree, a work of literature goes beyond and through them, as a form that more or less contingent historical meanings come to fill by turns."[44]

The reversal that replaces rationality with imagination and emotion as guides for dealing with reality also translates into a more effective understanding of human relations. Philosophers have doubted for a long time already that human actions are only or even primarily guided by reason. Whitehead proposed, for example, that "the basis of experience is emotional; knowledge is really an abstraction from affective relationships."[45] In addition to eliminating a misleading pretense, such a view has the advantage of recognizing the primacy of community over an individual's will in the determination of values. It recognizes the involvement of an individual as a whole thinking and feeling organism within a community and is predicated on the goal of achieving a "harmony of intellect and affect." Recognizing that "the satisfactions of understanding are bound up with the mysterious workings of imagination, which enlist both feelings and instincts that ultimately connect us to the world," it also contributes to radically alter traditional notions of what makes humans adapt to their environment.[46]

Within the context of social existence, the reversal translates into a concern for the evidence of social experience rather than the being of the social actors. Thus reason finds itself further demystified as a result of the subject's disintegration: as an essential element of human nature, it was a constitutive element of the individual's essence. It can now be seen as a pattern that structures collective thinking, thus constituting a grammar of experience through which individuals are expected to filter the real. Contrary to what humanisms of various kinds have proposed, reason belongs less to the individual than to society.

One of the notable achievements of poststructuralist criticism was to draw attention to the subterfuge of humanistic descriptions of mental processes. Todd May explains: "By undercutting the pretensions of humanism, poststructuralists hope to draw our attention to the many small, contingent, and often dispersed practices that contribute to who we are—and to our concept of ourselves as primarily self-constituting beings."[47] In this light, the autonomy of the subject is but a lure, a pretense that can occult the effective mechanism of reasons working in the interests of hidden designs or purposes. The theme of the subject's autonomy becomes a key factor in the deployment of the power to subject. According to François Dubet, when seen from a critical perspective he calls "post-Nietzschean," "the free subject of reason becomes nothing more than the representation of power, interiorized in the idea of the autonomous subject, in a belief in the reality of an individual who would be master of his/her Self. Modernity's and evolution's grand story is no longer that of emancipation and of knowledge—it is the story of subjection."[48] To bring that story to light, critics have replaced the theme of the subject's being by that of the subject's experience. This new perspective allows for a more nuanced and complex story to emerge. Dubet shows, for example, that the study of social experience leads to the realization that social systems are not reducible to a single logic or rationality and that individual and collective forms of behavior can coexist even when they are guided by heterogenous and divergent principles of action. As a result, we discover that "individuals do not fulfill a program but aim to construct a unity based on diverse elements of their social life and a multiplicity of orientations they carry within themselves. Thus social identity is not a 'being,' but a 'striving' [*travail*]."[49] Such a view obviously rejects the two extremes of individual voluntarism and social determinism and allows for a gap between individual action and social effect, recognizing that "there will always remain, in social experience, something unfinished and opaque because there is no absolute adequation between the actor's subjectivity and the objectivity of the system."[50]

An action can therefore be defined as both "a subjective orientation *and* a relation," since it can be oriented in terms of several, often competing, principles of communal or individual activity.[51] Furthermore, a community can define itself in terms of different and competing principles of cohesion such as national, local, or ethnic traditions. At the same time, these rationales are opposed by the ethic of the marketplace, which is international in orientation, and the philosophy of individualism promoted by popular culture. As a consequence, one is neither subjected completely to one's environment, nor can one gain an objective grasp of it: "Actors neither experience an immediate adhesion nor provide a pure testimony because they always reconstruct a distance in relation to themselves."[52] Moreover, this gap in an individual's perception of his or her self and of society is not so much a distance that alienates as a buffer zone that provides the opportunity to construct one's subjectivity. Dubet defines alienation "as the deprivation of the capacity to be a subject."[53] Subjectivity is thus construed as an essential component of the social experience, which "is constructed on the basis of a principle of subjectivization. The difficulty today comes from the fact that this principle no longer refers to any transcendence, to any nonsocial realm: the reconciliation of experience is not achieved in terms of God, of Reason, of history, of a value, of a norm, or of a social movement that would allow us to slide over the gap between society and individual experience."[54] The loss of transcendental themes is replaced by the realization that subjectivity can be constructed in the context of relations with others because, as we have already seen, the social subject finds its definition through "a play of tensions, through a labor and not through being."[55]

The subject, it turns out, is neither predestined nor preprogrammed. It is a view that characterizes the latest, postmodern approaches of philosophers and sociologists; it is an understanding that is also reinforced by what the scientific community is discovering about our neurological and genetic makeup. Even the scientists who study the DNA do not argue for resolving the age-old opposition between free will and determinism and provide, instead, further reasons for maintaining ambiguity and reciprocity in the opposition of our urges to determine our limits and to transcend them:

> All that human beings have created, all of culture and history, is the result and the record of that argument, that urge, one that continues to inform and shape us even as we go on reshaping it. We are each, then, indecipherable amalgams of our genes and of the influences of the environment and culture that our genes compelled us to create. It's a constant, variable exchange, a to-and-fro that continually affects in shifting and cyclical measures our physical and psychological states, and makes each of us, in the end, as unknowable as the make up of our very next thought, or walk, or days.[56]

What counts most then is the argument itself and the possibility for conducting it freely and openly. Examining the skeptical tradition in western philosophy, David Hiley distinguishes between two basic types of philosophical approaches. One, the "epistemology-centered philosophy" has always been concerned with establishing a secure foundation for philosophical inquiry "in order to guarantee that knowledge accurately represents reality." The other is an "edifying philosophy" that resists any attempt at imposing closure and privileging a particular method of inquiry: "The edifying philosophers are thus agreeing with Lessing's choice of the infinite *striving for* truth over 'all of Truth.' The goal of inquiry on this view is to keep inquiry going, 'to see keeping a conversation going as a sufficient aim of philosophy, to see wisdom as consisting in the ability to sustain a conversation.'"[57] It is perhaps in this sense that the postmodern age is revalorizing an ethos that has most commonly been associated with the Age of Enlightenment. We have seen already that it was the interference of "reality," of the evidence of disarray, suffering, and chaos around us that revealed the insufficiency of established systems of meaning. The evidence of the immediate brought out the illusory nature of all attempts at mediating—that is, validating, justifying, rationalizing—our experience of the world around us. It is, once more, the experience of Candide invalidating the systematic explanations of Pangloss.

I begin therefore with Voltaire. What is of particular interest for our time, I argue, is an attitude exemplified by some of Voltaire's works, an approach that could properly—though paradoxically—be called postmodern: it is the propensity for testing all our theorizing in the light of raw experience. Voltaire's stubborn insistence that all pronouncements of a general or abstract nature about the meaning of our existence, our selves, or our world be confronted with the unadulterated evidence of our experience is akin to a skepticism marking our own age.[58] I use the theme of travel as it is elaborated in Voltaire's *Contes* to further illustrate this point. Voltaire's attitude, in this regard, can also be taken as an important characteristic of the age: it is the propensity for the valuing of openness over closure, of indecision over truth.

At the same time, we need to recognize a basic weakness this approach shared with the spirit of the times. Thus, Voltaire's commonsensical notion of enlightened reason had to rely on a concept of *l'homme* to establish its validity. We now realize, of course, that one of the worst ways to begin a project purporting to understand or even to change the world or society is to base it on a definition of "man." In light of critiques elaborated by poststructuralist and postmodernist thinkers, such projects can only be relegated today to the history of delusions that trace the evolution of Western civilization. Truth is no longer to be found in a human essence or a human nature. As Barry Allen argues in his essay *Truth in Philosophy*: "With being, presence, and self-identical unity deferred *ad infinitum*, the value of truth can and must be 'reinscribed' where it belongs: 'in more powerful, larger, more stratified . . . interpretive contexts'—in other words, in the institutional-social practice where truth always was anyway, even when philosophers preferred to avert their eyes from time, history, and contingency and dream of True Being."[59] These projects of reinscription in different interpretive contexts are what constitute the work of a good number of thinkers today. Society has thus replaced nature as the ultimate frame of reference; existence in society has replaced the notion of an abstract being. The truth of the individual—or the subject, is no longer related to the unifying truth of nature; it finds itself fragmented along the multiple patterns created by processes of social integration and cultural adaptation. The subject finds itself at the mercy of forces and effects that constitute it according to relatively autonomous and heterogenous systems of logic. Consequently, it is no longer a question of understanding the actions of a subject from the perspective of some internal truth or in terms of a self-representation or self-reconstitution: it is a matter of analyzing the subject's constitution from the perspective of the individual's experience—as we saw earlier. As a result, as Susan Bordo points out, contemporary critical approaches are predicated on a fundamental reversal: "The knower, not the known, now comes under scrutiny—and not, as Descartes scrutinized the knower, for those contaminating elements which must be purged from cognition, but for those 'active and interpretive forces,' as Nietzsche says, 'through which alone seeing becomes seeing *something.*'"[60]

In chapter 2, I examine the theoretical strategy that has proven to be most effective in disclosing the elements and conditions that attend our ways of perceiving—the hermeneutical approach.

One of the reasons for the importance and prestige hermeneutics has gained as a critical approach, is its capacity for restoring the sociohistorical context overseeing the formation of past and present modes of understanding. Hermeneutical approaches can also help us gauge the critical distance separating us from the aspirations implicit in the Cartesian project. To put it in terms of a simple contrast: while Descartes was intent on eliminating a subjective bias in the name of Reason, hermeneutics teaches us to accept prejudice as the inevitable and necessary component of all systems of belief—especially those operating behind the pretense of Reason. And it helps disclose the particular subject whose interests are served by the promotion of an allegedly objective Reason—of "this highly abstract mode of thought, separable, in principle, from the emotional complexities and practical demands of ordinary life."[61] As Genevieve Lloyd shows, the veil of a rational and undistorted thought has mainly served to further reinforce the masculine bias inherent in Western culture and the radicalness with which Descartes effectuated "his separation of the ultimate requirements of truth-seeking from the practical affairs of everyday life reinforced already existing distinctions between male and female roles."[62] Accordingly, Reason's blindness to its own reasons stands out most glaringly in Western philosophy's elevation of the masculine at the expense of the feminine. The work of Michèle Le Doeuff effectively demonstrates that, hidden behind the pretense of an objective and universal Reason is the inherently masculine bias of philosophy. She also shows that to achieve its status and prerogatives, philosophy has had to rely on a strategy that contradicts its assertion of logical and rational procedure: it regularly has recourse to the imaginary whenever reason and logic fail it. Chapter 3 is devoted to Le Doeuff's remarkable critical project.

Another, by now well-documented instance in which Reason has served as a cover for special interests is the appropriation of the ideology of the Enlightenment in Western political theory and practice. Both Michel Foucault and the Frankfurt School thinkers have elaborated most telling critiques of this central tenet of Modernity's ethos. The School's two best-known representatives, Adorno and Horkheimer, have used a dialectical approach to devastating effect in revealing the self-canceling nature of such notions as Reason, Progress, and the Enlightenment. In Chapter 4, I survey the implications as well as the shortcomings of Adorno's and Horkheimer's dialectic by contrasting it with Foucault's genealogical method. Chapter 5 examines in greater detail Foucault's own approach to the whole question of the Enlightenment.

One of the notable legacies of the Enlightenment was the notion of a transcendental reason, which, as Lawrence Cahoone points out, became an important component of Western political theory—of liberalism in particular, "and was therefore embedded in Western politics, jurisprudence, and economic theory." It was a concept that required, as its corollary, a particular idea of the human capacity for responsible political involvement. As a consequence, "the notion that every individual mind is capable of perceiving both reality and universal, 'self-evident' moral-political truths, and capable of rational discourse, was written into the American Constitution as well as the *Critique of Pure Reason*."[63] It is an idea so familiar as to make it second-nature in Western ways of thinking about society and politics. What is not as well-known, is that this idea served also as the guiding inspiration for the Constitution of the USSR. Indeed, the Soviet Constitution is one of the most explicit and thorough statements of the hopes and confidence the Enlightenment bore for the emancipation of humankind.[64] In this regard, of course, the Constitution of the USSR also turns out to be one of the great hoaxes in the history of humankind since all of the rights and freedoms it so scrupulously enumerates were systematically and rigorously denied its citizens. Consequently, the collapse of the Soviet Union is arguably the most spectacular failure of a project undertaken under the aegis of modernity's premises. The fall of *homo sovieticus* represents thus the ruin of one of modernity's most ambitious attempts at realizing a utopian concept of the human. What is perhaps most remarkable about this project of remaking humanity is the tenacity and durability of the pretense—especially in light of the unrelenting application of terror and repression that became the distinguishing feature of the Soviet experiment. The institution of the gulag is, in this regard, the most dramatic symptom of the project's inherent duplicity and the writings of its victims provide us with a precious testimony to one of the bleakest episodes in the history of humanity. Chapter 6 considers the implications of this episode through the memoirs of one of the victims.

At the same time, and paradoxically, the literature of the gulag reveals that the collapse of this experiment at redesigning human beings according to a universal model was accompanied by the emergence of old and familiar forms of human identity that sought their validation in themes that had officially been banned. Faced with the threat of annihilation, the victims of the gulag sought—and continue to seek—solace and redemption in a solidarity offered by communal, cultural, and ethnic spheres of identification. In this sense, it is a literature that not only marks our age but even more the peoples and the countries whose experience it reflects. It is a literature, in other words, that serves to define not only a moment in the history of civilization but even more to shape the identity of those who lived through this profoundly dehumanizing episode. In chapter 7, I survey the literature of deportation of Latvia, my country of origin, and try to situate it at a juncture that marks the transition between two eras—between the disintegration of a pretense of civilization and attempts to define anew a collective identity.

1

Voltaire and the
Limits of Reason

There are, generally speaking, two opposite viewpoints concerning the extent to which we are still beholden to an ideology derived from the Enlightenment. According to one viewpoint, the Enlightenment project is still valid and, though its aspirations are yet to be realized, its goals are still worthy of guiding our thinking and our actions. The other viewpoint holds that the project is no longer relevant because the terms within which it was conceived are hardly applicable in the context of present-day concerns and insights. According to this perspective, attempts to implement such an ideology can only lead to various forms of delusion and the result is at best a pretense masking the play of power and privilege that sustains contemporary socio-economic systems. In this light, it becomes apparent that the value system we have inherited from the eighteenth century is an abstraction that is no longer sustained by the faith in humanity and its destiny that gave the system its legitimacy in the eighteenth century. As David Hiley points out, "Our problem in the twentieth century is that we have inherited the Enlightenment conception of the connection between the growth of knowledge and the improvement of ourselves and society, as well as the Enlightenment conceptions of reason, autonomy, and hope for ourselves and the future, yet we have rejected the metaphysical structure and teleological conception of history that made the Enlightenment view plausible."[1] Paradoxically, it may well be the very success of the Enlightenment project that is responsible for its own downfall. As we saw earlier, such fundamental categories as Reason and Nature have lost much of their

19

credibility; thus the critical thrust of the ideas spawned by the Enlightenment ended up invalidating the very foundations that made them possible. Lawrence Cahoone proposes the following explanation:

> The interpretive categories that have shepherded modernity's achievements have succeeded so well that they have shattered the interpretive context that was essential to early modernity. The result is that in the twentieth century modernity has suffered a *de-contextualization* of its basic interpretive categories. The beliefs and modes of interpretation that once provided a context and a source of mediation for modernity's fundamental conceptions of subjectivity and objectivity have been delegitimated. This loss of context and mediation has affected the conceptions of subjectivity and objectivity themselves. Without a medium of relation their nature is drastically changed.[2]

For eighteenth-century philosophers, the two principal conceptual categories used as guides for thought were reason and nature. While these concepts were to become absolute and take the place, in effect, of a Divine principle, the uses to which reason in particular was put in the eighteenth century were sufficiently tinged with skepticism to make them comparable to present-day postmodern approaches—as I have already argued elsewhere.[3] For the purposes of the present study, what needs to be ascertained more precisely is the functioning of reason in light of the distinction made earlier between philosophies seeking to guarantee knowledge of reality and those questioning it. To do this, I return once more to Voltaire, the most eminent spokesperson for the Age of Reason. The contexts I have chosen for highlighting the uses and conceptualization of reason in Voltaire are the themes of *pays* and *dépaysement*: that is, I wish to contrast the positive notion of belonging, of being circumscribed by one's provincial locale to the negative idea of uprooting, of estrangement.

In a similar manner, Voltairean reason also partakes of two general aspects—one positive, the other negative. On the positive side, reason is to be understood as the ordering principle that makes us feel at home in the universe. Voltaire's intellectual activity implies the postulate of a rational order ruling the universe: it is an order outside history, founded in nature, and is the basis for

Voltaire's optimistic or melioristic outlook. This faith in reason manifests itself as an intuitive certitude: "God has implanted in us a principle of reason that is universal, as he has given feathers to birds and skins to bears; and this principle is so immutable that it subsists in spite of all the passions which oppose it, in spite of those tyrants who would drown it in blood, in spite of the impostors who want to annihilate it through superstition."[4] Reason is thus one of those principles that is necessary to make sense of the world. The trouble is that the world and human actions frequently do not make sense—it is in this regard that reason acquires a critical responsibility and is used as a defense mechanism against everything that threatens a rational conceptualization of the world. For Voltaire then, as Didier Masseau explains, "there is an ethics of reason: seen as a shared demand of sense and unity, it provides a defense against enthusiasm, passions that divide, and the spirit of domination. It prevents recourse to the irrational when confronted by the inexplicable, because the impotence of human reason does not necessarily summon the supernatural."[5] Reason thus understood is aware of its own limitations and achieves its privilege and preeminence only by dint of this fundamental modesty it displays whenever it gauges its own potential and capacity. It is this fluctuation between certitude and doubt that marks the functioning of reason as it is revealed in the travels of the characters of Voltaire's philosophical tales.

The heroes of Voltaire's *Contes*, as we well know, are committed to traveling.[6] These travels may begin unexpectedly and are often undertaken unwillingly: Candide is sent forth "with great kicks in the behind"; Zadig has to flee from home because his life is in danger; the Princess of Babylon, following a misunderstanding, pursues her lover over the lands of three continents; Micromégas, banished from the court of Syrius after he publishes a controversial book, undertakes to visit other planets "to complete his education of mind and heart" (132). Though unwilling to leave home at first, Voltaire's voyagers end up recognizing the formative importance of their peregrinations. Candide, reflecting on the dramatic difference between Eldorado and his native Westphalia is certain that Pangloss would not have thought the castle of Thunder-ten-tronckh to be the best place on earth had he seen Eldorado and adds, as an afterthought, "It is clear that one should travel" (218). Zadig, who is already endowed with a philosophical disposition before his travails begin, is made even wiser by the experience they provide.

Even the Babylonian Princesses' lover, Amazan—who comes from a country where liberty, equality, cleanliness, abundance, and tolerance reign—discovers that other cultures may be superior to his in certain regards. Having received a map from an English geographer, he is surprised to see the world represented on a piece of paper and recognizes that "the Albionian, who had given him a gift of the universe in an abbreviated version, was not at all wrong in claiming that people were a thousand times better educated on the shores of the Thames than on those of the Nile, the Euphrates, or the Ganges" (490).

Thus, although they are driven to travel by circumstances outside their control, Voltaire's heroes are wanderers by nature and assimilate quite readily the lessons of their peripatetic experiences. Their outlook is often marked by restlessness, by a disposition to feel unsatisfied with their own country and culture. As a result, as Cacambo remarks, "When we don't have what we need in one world, we find it in another. It's a great pleasure to see and do new things" (207). This desire to travel for the pure pleasure of discovering new and different vistas is most evident in the case of l'Ingénu, in whom love of travel is inseparable from an inherent spontaneity of character. Relating to his newfound French friends the circumstances in which he came to England, he explains, very simply, "I have, by nature, a passion for seeing new places" (325).

The connection between character and travel is thus a given in Voltaire's philosophical tales. Consequently, there are evident parallels between physical displacement and intellectual movement and the change of scenery brings about a corresponding change on a psychological as well as a philosophical level. Which is to say that the most significant events taking place during the course of the travels undertaken by the principal characters of the *Contes* take place on an intellectual level. After Micromégas has become acquainted with the secretary of the Academy of Saturn, we are told that "they decide to take a little philosophical trip together" (136). Indeed, all of these voyages are first and foremost philosophical, as many commentators of Voltaire's *Contes* have already pointed out. It is also on this level that the reader is invited to take part in the adventures of Voltaire's heroes. The *dépaysement* experienced by the characters is a philosophical lesson that invites the reader to leave the comfort of his or her intellectual home and to consider other, different, sometimes strange and disquieting vistas that propose alternatives to ingrained habits of thought.

What is at stake in these travels, in the most general sense, is Reason. Reason, it could be argued, is both the vehicle and the object of the voyages. Voltaire uses Reason or, to put it differently, he appeals to certain standards of common sense and understanding while aiming to effectuate certain changes in our understanding and appreciation of this most universal of vehicles for thought. Noteworthy, as well, is the dual strategy adopted by Voltaire as he explores the ways of human understanding and rationalization: Reason acquires both a negative-critical and a positive-constructive thrust in its application. The critical force of Reason serves to diminish human vanity and brings out its own limitations by highlighting the deficiencies of human understanding. Voltaire's purpose, in this regard, is to place humans and their concerns in an appropriately philosophical perspective by demonstrating that the encounter with different forms of thought will inevitably contribute to break up limited views of the world. Communication, exchanges with others, therefore constitute an essential component for the process of intellectual *dépaysement* achieved by Voltaire's tales. In *Les Oreilles du comte de Chesterfield et le chapelain Goudman* (Count Chesterfield's Ears and the Chaplain Goudman), the surgeon Sidrac tells the priest Goudman, inviting him to dinner, "We will chat, and your thinking faculty will have the pleasure of communicating with mine by means of the spoken word, which is a marvelous thing humans don't admire enough" (674). Similarly, as they return to Europe, Candide and Martin pass the time by conversing: "They did not stop arguing for fifteen days, and at the end of fifteen days they were no further along than on the first. But at least they talked, they exchanged ideas, they consoled one another" (227).

Paradoxically then, communication does not necessarily lead to greater understanding but only ends up revealing the shortcomings of this essentially human faculty of reasoning. When Sidrac declares confidently that "we are in a century of reason; we find easily what appears as truth to us, and we dare say it," Goudman retorts: "I am afraid this truth may not be very much," and that while clear progress has been achieved in a field such as mathematics, the only thing endless discussions of metaphysical themes have uncovered is "our ignorance" (676). Likewise, when asked about the intellectual activities of earthlings, a philosopher informs Micromégas: "We dissect flies, . . . we measure lines, we assemble numbers, we agree on two or three points that we understand, and we argue about two or three thousand that we don't understand" (145).

The disproportion between the little that can be known with any confidence and the vast realm of the unknown and the unknowable is, of course, one of Voltaire's favorite themes. Thus the hermit reminds Zadig that "humans were wrong to pass judgment on a whole of which they could only see the smallest part" and that humans "judge everything without knowing anything" (80, 82). The mark of wisdom then is the Socratic capacity for recognizing and admitting one's ignorance. Micromégas and his traveling companion decide to go exploring the universe "after they had shared the little they knew and much of what they did not know" (135–36). In the tale *Le Taureau blanc* (The white bull), the wise old Mambrès, having lived thirteen hundred years, can only come to a pessimistic conclusion about the sum of his experiences: "I am very old, I have studied all my life, but I see a quantity of incompatibilities that I cannot reconcile. . . . All in all, I am beginning to suspect that this world is made up of contradictions" (577–78).

At the same time, it is at the point where ignorance is accepted as an incontrovertible fact of human existence that Reason acquires a positive force. This comes as a result of an ironic truth marking the human condition: the ultimate goal of traveling, the result of the process of *dépaysement* is the realization that one must still recognize a particular corner of the universe as one's own, as the ultimate destination for one's travels—a place which, in some cases, turns out to be the starting point. For Voltaire's heroes, following their multiple adventures and misadventures a certain sense of order is restored—"tout rentre dans l'ordre," as it were. What is achieved, in addition, is a sense of seeing the order of things in a different light. Such, for example, is the outcome of *Jeannot et Colin*. At the conclusion of the tale, Colin generously welcomes his friend back to the village after the latter's ambition to achieve success in Paris has ended in dismal failure: "You will return with me to our native land," Colin tells Jeannot. "I will teach you the business, it isn't very difficult; I will make you a partner, and we will live happily in the corner of this earth where we were born" (290). We recognize, in this invitation, the famous admonition to cultivate one's garden. It expresses the wisdom Candide only achieves at the end of his travels, although already in Eldorado, the king pointed out to him that one must necessarily settle somewhere and that he was foolish to leave: "I realize my country isn't much," the king remarks, "but, when one is tolerably well somewhere, one should stay there" (220). In *Le Monde comme il va* (The way things are in this world), the genie Ituriel, having decided to heed Babouc's recommendation that Persépolis not be annihilated, also concludes that it is futile to aspire to impossible ideals and that, in this world, "if everything is not right, everything is tolerable" (108).

The wisdom leading to a *pays* one can call one's own also enables the traveler to discover a certain universality of human needs and aspirations. After many travels through space Micromégas admits that, while he has seen many beings that are superior in terms of physical capability, "I saw none who did not have more desires than true needs, and more needs than satisfaction" (134). A kind of existential anguish or dissatisfaction thus is recognized as the common trait marking all forms of existence in the universe. Once one understands that it is not possible to assuage this anguish no matter how far or wide one travels, one is ready to live life on its own terms by simply accepting its unpredictability and vicissitudes. Following the ruin of dreams and illusions, there remains the resolve to make the best of the existing situation by concentrating on the practical and tangible aspects of life.The experience of *dépaysement* thus helps the travelers achieve what could be called a *dénuement*, a state of intellectual and moral lucidity that is only possible after delusions have dissipated and all pretenses have been cast aside. Once disabused of the false promises of life, the characters can develop fully their human potential. Hardship and disappointments are the most effective paths leading to these transformations. One place that is particularly conducive to a spiritual *dénuement* is prison, as demonstrated by l'Ingénu's experience. The visitor from North America takes advantage of his incarceration to complete his education. The time spent in prison is particularly profitable because l'Ingénu is an ideal student: free of prejudices, his mind is like Locke's *tabula rasa*, ready to assimilate the lessons of the books he reads and of the conversations he has with his cell-mate, the reformed Jansenist Gordon. As Voltaire points out, "Things entered his brain without a cloud" (332). L'Ingénu's education even proves beneficial to Gordon, who acquires a new, critical perspective on his own formation. Under the influence of this unexpected contact and example, the old Jansenist undergoes a gradual transformation, "the harshness of his former opinions left his heart; he was changed into a man, as was the Huron" (371). "What!" exclaims Gordon, struck by a disquieting realization, "I have spent fifty years educating myself and I fear that I will not be able to attain the natural good sense of this almost wild child! I am afraid I have diligently fortified prejudices; he only listens to simple nature" (354).

The meaning of nature is clearly paradoxical in this regard: nature does not represent a return to a more primitive state but stands for a precondition that gives access to a higher level of intelligence and awareness. It is a condition that permits the effective deployment and application of Reason. Zadig is a model for this ideal because he is a man, Voltaire tells us, "born with a beautiful natural disposition fortified by education" (30). Education is then the fulfillment of what is natural in humans. As Voltaire remarks about *L'Homme aux quarante écus* (The man with forty Ecus), "How much has monsieur André's good sense been fortified since he acquired a library!" (437). The *dénuement* achieved through this valorization of nature does not lead to ignorance but enhances one's capacity for enlightenment. After the various pretenses sustaining the vanity of ethnocentrisms and the blindness of superstitions have been dissipated, natural Reason can truly develop to its full potential, it becomes capable of illuminating the forces and conditions that serve to fortify prejudice and ignorance. The development of a natural common sense allows one to reject whatever is incomprehensible or claims to explain the unknowable. As the chaplain Goudman remarks, "It is, when you think about it, ridiculous to utter words one doesn't understand, and to believe in beings one cannot know in the slightest" (676). History teaches us that entire nations can be kept in a state of barbarism and ignorance when an obsession with metaphysical themes passes for wisdom: "Everything was subverted when discussions were about unintelligible things: everything fell into place again as soon as such considerations were scorned," explains a member of parliament as he relates the history of England to Amazan (488).

Reason can thus provide a critical perspective on the world. By developing an unaffected commonsensical approach, one can discern the incoherence and folly of human ways. On sighting the coast of England, Candide asks Martin, "Are they as crazy there as in France?" To which Martin replies, "It's another kind of madness" (237). No matter what the country, human existence is distorted by a very human propensity to lie about everything, to misrepresent reality. The noble Venetian Pococuranté observes: "It is beautiful to write what one believes; this is the privilege of humanity. In all of Italy, we only write what we don't believe; those who live in the country of the Caesars and Antonines dare not have a single idea without the permission of a Jacobin" (245). Similarly, in England, freedom of expression is vitiated by "partisan passion and spirit" (245). But it is the French and their institutions that provide Voltaire with the most striking examples of incoherence—of barbaric mores parading under the pretense of civilized refinement. Shortly after their arrival in France, Martin tells Candide: "Imagine all possible contradictions, all incompatibilities, you will see them in the government, in the tribunals, in the churches, in the spectacles of this weird nation" (231). The natural reason of Voltaire's heroes helps bring out the contradictions. Having learned by heart the sacred text that provides Europeans with the moral guidelines for living, l'Ingénu is forced to come to a simple conclusion: "I notice every day that people do here an infinite number of things that aren't in your book, and none of the things it tells them to do" (338). By presenting civilized refinement from the perspective of a natural rationality, Voltaire achieves a reversal of values; thus, l'Ingénu concludes, "My American compatriots would never have treated me with the barbarism I have experienced; they cannot imagine it. They are called *savages*; they are indeed uncouth, but the people in this country are refined scoundrels" (349).

Voltaire's satire of his compatriots is particularly savage in *La princesse de Babylone*. The princess observes that social and cultural life in Paris is determined by a fundamental distinction between the two social categories of the "oisifs" and the "occupés." While the idlers are preoccupied with the arts and entertainment the capital has to offer, the busy ones ensure the functioning of the governing institutions of the country. What stands out, as a result, is the contrast between the two groups and, "the more the idlers were polite, pleasant, and likable, the more one could note a sad contrast between them and the assemblies of the busy ones" (495). Prominent among the latter is "a troop of somber fanatics, half-absurd, half-crooked," as well as a number of "guardians of ancient barbaric customs." Because of a blind adherence to ancient barbaric customs, "there was no proportion between crimes and punishment" and, notes the princess, "in the city of pleasure, there still existed horrible customs." Whenever injustice occurs or atrocities are committed in the name of justice, the idlers are momentarily concerned but quickly return to their favorite activities: "They made shrill noises but the next day they no longer thought of it and only spoke of the latest fashions" (496).

It is thus a society in which everything has been turned upside down: ignorance is wisdom and social status is reflected in one's parasitic existence, not in one's usefulness. When he arrives in Paris, Jeannot receives his first lesson in life from an author described as a "pleasant ignoramus" and who proposes a fundamental truth to his pupil, namely that "respectable people (I mean those who are very rich) know everything without having learned anything." This is because "in the long run, they learn to evaluate everything they order and pay for" (286). Jeannot learns very quickly and in no time "acquired the art of speaking without understanding himself and perfected the habit of being good for nothing" (287). Thus, while the hedonism of the idlers thrives under the cover of literary and artistic brilliance, it is actually underwritten by ignorance, since it is wealth that determines the value of anything. This brilliant but empty-headed society legitimates itself by means of a circular logic. When a conviction becomes entrenched, it becomes a prejudice that is self-perpetuating because it accepts "what is" as a law that suffices unto itself and rejects any evidence that might undermine the security of apodictic truths. That is why the promotion of a natural Reason is so important. As Sétoc suggests bitterly to Zadig, "Is there anything more respectable than an ancient outrage?" To which Zadig simply replies, "Reason is more ancient still" (57).

At the same time, while Voltaire posits reason as a basic nature that determines human capacity for thought, he does not deem it to be the infallible instrument that it was for Descartes, for example. In a dialogue between a philosopher and nature, Voltaire has the philosopher emit the following supposition: "There must be an eternal geometer who guides you, a supreme intelligence presiding over your operations." To which, nature replies: "You are right; I am water, earth, fire, atmosphere, metal, mineral, stone, vegetation, animal. I do sense there is an intelligence in me; you have one too, you don't see it. I don't see mine either; I feel this invisible power, I cannot know it: how could you, you who are but a small part of me, know what I don't know?"[7] The point at which one has to arrive before applying reason effectively then, is the understanding of its fundamental deficiency and limitations. That is because the lack inherent in human reason is not a motive for despair or apathy but a most powerful incentive for action. We find this attitude exemplified by the restless spirit of the heroes of Voltaire's *Contes*, who relate each experience to a whole context of prejudices and expectations that is both posited and questioned in the process. They are thus able to remain alert to the gap separating the known from the unknown and themselves from the world. The themes expressing this context—the place of humans in society or in the universe, the laws ordering the universe—whatever their initial configuration, gradually become modified with the new understanding each experience brings.

One way to reconcile ourselves with the world then is to spin tales about it. As "le bon vieillard Mambrès" observes, "It is only by telling tales that one succeeds in this world" (581). But fables can be of various sorts and can be told for various purposes. Having read a number of books on ancient history, l'Ingénu is able to establish the following preferences: "I like the fables of philosophers, I laugh at those of children, and I hate those of impostors" (353). These distinctions are revealing. Children's fables exorcise the unknown by eliciting imaginary realms of magic and wonder. The fables of impostors are fabrications claiming the status of truth in order to maintain established areas of privilege and to preserve the comforts of conventional convictions. They are not be simply despised or ignored, however; to deconstruct their capacity for obscuring people's minds, they need to be retold from the perspective of more enlightening horizons provided by the experience of the world. It is this recasting that constitutes the critical power of Voltaire's narrative, in which, as René Pomeau remarks, "as soon as they are enunciated, the pretenses of humans submerge into ridicule" (128).

As for the fables of the philosophers, especially of the genre inaugurated by Voltaire, their merit is to make us realize that the process of understanding our place in the world is never-ending. Voltaire's procedure, in this regard, can properly be viewed as a hermeneutical one. It is guided by the realization that our understanding is not subject to immutable laws so much as it is molded by a long development of historical antecedents. That is why we can never rise above or escape the conditions that have given shape to our thought but must strive to remain constantly open to a universe that is properly hermeneutical in nature. As Hans-Georg Gadamer explains, since reason exists for us only in concrete, historical terms, "the finite nature of one's own understanding is the manner in which reality, resistance, the absurd, and the unintelligible assert themselves." Consequently, present-day theoreticians of hermeneutics, just as Voltaire's heroes, find that a permanent state of dissatisfaction, of inauthenticity is the signal mark of such an opening to the world. Heidegger calls this condition *Unheimlichkeit*, a sense of not-being-at-home in the world. It is a sense of alienation that impels us to seek a reconciliation between our existence and the unknown around us and to confront what we think we know with the evidence provided by our experience. An awareness of the *décalage* separating these two kinds of evidence gives rise to new insights. As Paul Ricoeur explains, interpretation takes place "at the hinge between linguistics and nonlinguistics, between language and lived experience."[9] The insights that we discover fail to provide definitive answers, of course. And Gadamer reminds us that "our desire and capacity to understand always go beyond any statement we can make."[10] But this lack is also what gives fiction its powers of conviction. Voltaire's tales clearly speak of such a desire and reflect a creative capacity for suggesting more than can be said. While bringing into question the limits of our capacity for establishing securely the meaning of our existence, Voltaire's ironic treatment of civilization's shortcomings thus underlines an attitude akin to our own postmodern sensibilities. Voltaire's purpose was to promote a rationality that would be guided and tested by the practical demands of the world. He understood, at the same time, that the practices that make up the social world are not necessarily guided by the rationality that governs discourses.

In other important ways, of course, Voltaire's thought epitomizes the modernist aspirations of his age. As he combated the evils caused by human ignorance and superstition, Voltaire hoped to clear the way for a rational social order, conceptualized in accordance with a transcendent notion of an orderly and rational universe. He was thus helping to set in place the principles that eventually became entrenched in modern social thought.

With time, and following the imperceptible transformation of the sociohistoric conditions that gave rise to these notions, the truths that were self-evident have turned into free-floating abstractions. They have undergone the common fate of discursive constructs that have forgotten their nondiscursive corollaries. Voltaire's well-meaning attempt at promoting a rational outlook on life in society has produced what one critic of Western civilization identifies as "Voltaire's bastards": these are "the central concepts upon which we operate [and that] were long ago severed from their roots and changed into formal rhetoric. They have no meaning. They are used wildly or administratively as masks."[11]

The principal shortcoming of Voltaire's philosophical undertaking is to be found in the premise on which he based it. In this regard, Voltaire's procedure could be considered as belonging to a long and respectable philosophical tradition. Thus, when we examine the history of philosophy, we can see that "to get out of difficulty, philosophers generally have recourse to a sovereign expedient, which is to postulate that the universe in which humans evolve is simple and orderly."[12] Likewise, for Voltaire, the world was basically uncomplicated—though largely unknowable—and he trusted Reason to justify this conviction. While he recognized the shortcomings of Reason, it could be argued that his skepticism did not take him far enough. What Voltaire did not recognize was Reason's more nihilistic side, which is its power to negate itself. It has become evident, for example, that Reason cannot both be ethical and instrumental: it cannot be, at the same time, a human nature or ethical essence *and* a capacity for shaping nature or the world. The more Reason places means of control and domination in the hands of humans, the more they tend to valorize and legitimate ethically these means. As a result, the system of domination tends to acquire a life of its own, frequently negating whatever justification Reason provided it at the outset.

But then, Voltaire can hardly be blamed for failing to anticipate developments that were to take place in the following century. While, eventually, the world of experience will fail to live up to the Enlightenment standard of Reason and Western philosophy will come to a point where, according to Joan Stambaugh, it "seems to have exhausted its capacity to produce a new vision of reality," the problems Voltaire faced seemed real enough and the reason he conceptualized adequate for the critical purposes he thought important.[13] As discrepancies between Reality and Reason became more apparent, Voltaire's tempered skepticism inevitably gave way to more radical ways of questioning the reasons behind Reason and its ways of representing the world.

2

The Postmodern Outlook
for Hermeneutics

As our society's ideological modes of self-justification have been increasingly brought into question, a number of its cherished cultural and political alibis have come unglued. The notion of the individual is beginning to appear as little more than an imaginary construct whose reality is enhanced through the manipulation of desire and whose alleged essence has proven useful for assigning blame and responsibility. The theme of a democratic system of law and order has become a useful cover for institutional and political strategies that seek to validate self-serving agendas.

Notions ensuring the cohesion of the socioeconomic system are thus in a disarray—not because they have been betrayed, as some have claimed, but because we are beginning to realize they have no tangible or convincing referents. It is becoming increasingly evident that the terminology bequeathed to us by the discourse of the Enlightenment has been used to create an abstract conceptual realm whose function, in turn, has been to mislead: it has served as a metaphysical foundation for socioeconomic forces that are free to develop their own peculiar logic and rationales.

This state of affairs has provided a fertile ground for critical discourses aiming to discern the nature and results of the cultural and ideological disintegration marking the second half of the twentieth century. One of the most effective critical strategies has been the hermeneutical approach—especially of the Heideggerian and Gadamerian variety. It is an approach that effectuates a reversal in the habits of thought we have inherited from the Enlightenment: it teaches us to consider interpretation—not as a means for elaborat-

33

ing an original and unpublished form of comprehension, but as the method with which we can elucidate an already existing state of comprehension and thus discern the acquired habits and preformed standards that constitute our understanding of "reality."

Since the time of the Ancient Greeks, when it first came into use, the concept of hermeneutics has undergone changes that are both considerable and revealing. They are revealing because each age seems to elaborate the hermeneutical strategy that is best suited to its particular needs. These requirements, in turn, are defined to a large extent by each era's preeminent practitioners of the art of hermeneutics, the theoreticians whose work evolves within the boundaries set by a long tradition—even as it attempts to overcome these limits. The practice of interpretation is thus characterized by the twofold orientation of its responsiveness to present needs and past precedents. Theorists of interpretation generally realize that, to be hermeneutically responsible, they must inevitably refer to the tradition from which they gain their affiliation and identity. They acknowledge the paradoxical relationship hermeneutical thinking maintains with its antecedents by underlining its dependency on a tradition it has to recognize as insuperable, even as it attempts to evade or overthrow this legacy.

Thus, our present understanding and practice of hermeneutics is still perhaps best related to the thinking of Montaigne, who "articulates a line of inquiry inextricably inscribed in a certain epistemological and metaphysical tradition of Western thought."[1] As Jean Starobinski has shown, one of Montaigne's signal merits is to have demonstrated the precarious nature of identity. Identity, for Montaigne, was not to be found in an essence hidden behind a veil of appearances but was to be discovered in the appearances themselves, that is, in relations involving the world—which is, after all, a world of appearances. For Montaigne, explains Starobinski, "Identity is no longer a tacit acquiescence of the same in the same, which strengthens and confirms the innermost self; rather it includes and maintains difference, it accepts the risks of appearing, of becoming, and of language."[2] In this regard, Montaigne inaugurated a line of thought that was opposed to claims made in the name of the seemingly timeless desire for absolute knowledge, an urge to make "present the fundamental unity or ground of knowledge and understanding through the unveiling of *Self-evident* first principles and truths."[3] It is a desire that manifests itself as a search for unshakable principles of reference, signification, and identity. In this regard, the notable achievement of a hermeneutical approach has been to disclose and to question the presumption behind such a desire: "The ideal object of this desire—'truth,' metaphysical 'first principles' of 'self' and 'God,' the Kantian 'thing-in-itself,' or Husserlian transcendental conditions—is presumed to stand outside or independent of the linguistic framework, the interpretive context in which it is *re-presented.'*"[4]

The pattern of opposition and resistance to claims made in the name of certain and verifiable truths achieved its fullest elaboration in the nineteenth century. Thus, Schleiermacher was to reject the fundamental principle motivating the Cartesian quest for self-centered certitude by arguing that "every individual is developed through his language, and that therefore every understanding of an individual discourse requires a substantial understanding of language."[5] Moreover, Schleiermacher stipulated, the understanding of language is not available directly or immediately because it is *discourse* that connects individuals to language; consequently, understanding develops in the context of a relation, it is the actualization of an intelligibility that has already been articulated: "Hermeneutics is the art of relating discourse [*Reden*] and understanding [*Verstehen*] to each other."[6]

In the twentieth century this line of thinking was to be pursued most notably by Martin Heidegger, who introduces a new approach to the highly problematic notion of Being in philosophic debate by making the ordinary, commonsensical awareness-of-being dependent on an already preconstituted dimension of being. Heidegger draws the insightful distinction between the ineffable awareness of Being and a concrete consciousness of being-in-the-world. Furthermore, he proposes that, while both awarenesses are clearly distinct, they are also and inevitably related because being-in-the-world is seen as a projection of the primordial sense of Being on the objects constituting the world. These objects are not created as objects of knowledge but reveal themselves as elements, as the parts of an understanding that was always already motivated by the quest for understanding; consequently, "in interpretation, understanding does not become something different. It becomes itself."[7] The act of understanding is not an appropriation made possible by a preconstituted and self-sufficient consciousness—as it is for Descartes, for example: "In interpreting, we do not, so to speak, throw a 'signification' over some naked thing which is present-at-hand, we do not stick a value on it; but when something within-the-world is encountered as such, the thing in question already has an involvement which is disclosed in our understanding of the world, and this involvement is one which gets laid out by the interpretation [*die durch die Auslegung herausgelegt vird*]."[8] All acts of interpretation have to be seen therefore as grounded in a capacity to see and to conceptualize that is already given in advance: "Any interpretation which is to contribute understanding, must already have understood what is to be interpreted."[9]

Heidegger thus elaborates what was to become perhaps the most influential version of the hermeneutic circle—the self-referential process of understanding from which it is not possible to escape. Nevertheless, this circle is not to be viewed as a trap, according to Heidegger, because it does not condemn us to an endlessly repeated gesture that has no option but to duplicate itself ad infinitum. As Heidegger explains, the circle "is not to be reduced to the level of a vicious circle, or even of a circle to be tolerated." On the contrary, the awareness of circularity should make us realize that "our first, last, and constant task is never to allow our fore-having, fore-sight, and fore-conception to be presented to us by fancies and popular conceptions, but rather to make the scientific theme secure by working out the forestructures in terms of the things themselves."[10] Hermeneutics imposes an awareness that is also a responsibility, an intellectual ethos whose basic principle is to question and reject all convictions gained through the seemingly spontaneous productions of common sense. Or, at most, a commonsensical attribution has to be taken as just one of the meanings generated by discourse.

Heidegger distinguishes also between *ein Geredetes als solches*—the meaning a discourse carries in the context of the discursive configuration to which it belongs, and *das Gesagte als solches*—which is the meaning intended to be imparted, meant to be transmitted by the discourse. In other words, what the discourse is about is first and foremost its own articulation or imbrication in a general discursive pattern that is subject to historical determinants and cultural conditions. Moreover, the two levels of meaning do not necessarily connect in any way: "That which the discourse is *about* [*das Worüber der Rede*] does not necessarily or even for the most part serve as the theme for an assertion in which one gives something a definite character. . . . What the discourse is about is a structural item that it necessarily possesses; for discourse helps to constitute the disclosedness of Being-in-the-world, and in its own structure it is modeled upon this basic state of Dasein."[11]

Hans-Georg Gadamer provides a further elaboration on the Heideggerian insights into the process of interpretation. Gadamer is especially interested in investigating the dimension that has already prepared and predisposed us to perceive, understand, and judge before we are even aware of being engaged in the processes of perception, comprehension, and evaluation. Gadamer proposes, therefore, that "it is not so much our judgments as it is our prejudices that constitute our being."[12] Also, just as Heidegger insisted on the positive and constructive aspects of the circularity marking the interpretive process, Gadamer views prejudice not as detrimental, but as necessary. Prejudices, he explains, "are biases of our openness to the world. They are simply conditions whereby we experience something—whereby what we encounter says something to us."[13] It is also this realization that brings out the ontological importance of hermeneutics because it makes us see interpretation as inherently constitutive of our very being in the world: "The way that we experience one another, the way that we experience historical tradition, the way that we experience the natural givenness of our existence and of our world, constitutes a truly hermeneutic universe, in which we are not imprisoned, as if behind insurmountable barriers, but to which we are opened."[14] To preserve this openness, it is essential that we avoid a temptation that works to negate the promise of a hermeneutical understanding: it is the temptation to make hermeneutics into a science, to engage in an effort to discover immutable laws of interpretation that would simply naturalize our prejudices. Gadamer finds that we need to be particularly aware of this danger today: "I feel that we are living in a state of constant overstimulation in our historical consciousness. It is a consequence of this overstimulation and, as I hope to show, a bad short-circuit if one reacts to this over-estimation of historical change by invoking the eternal order of nature and summoning the naturalness of man to legitimate the idea of natural law."[15] Our understanding is not subject to laws as much as it is shaped by a long development of historical antecedents. That is why we can never rise above or escape the conditions that have given shape to our understanding: "Understanding is never subjective behavior toward a given 'object,' but towards its effective history—the history of its influence; in other words, understanding belongs to the being of that which is understood."[16]

The Cartesian paradigm has thus been completely reversed: no longer the initiator, no longer in charge of its encounter with reality, the subject has instead become dependent on the object of its cogitation. In light of Gadamer's explanation, the self-assuredness of the *Cogito* becomes, in effect, a pseudounderstanding, a self-delusion. Moreover, this deficiency cannot be overcome, and it is in this regard that a hermeneutical approach stands clearly opposed to a critique of ideology. As Paul Ricoeur explains: "The gesture of hermeneutics is a humble one of acknowledging the historical conditions to which all human understanding is subsumed in the reign of finitude; that of the critique of ideology is a proud gesture of defiance directed against the distortions of human communication."[17] At the same time, Ricoeur finds that a confrontation between hermeneutics and the critique of ideology is both revealing and useful because it offers a way of testing the validity of the claims entertained by the two approaches. He therefore proceeds to examine the well-known critique Jürgen Habermas has elaborated of the hermeneutical approach in general and of Gadamer's work in particular.

Ricoeur points out, first, that the Habermasian tactic rests on two main assumptions: one is the premise that knowledge is inevitably distorted by special interests whose purpose is to maintain relations marked by domination and inequality; a second thesis proposes that it is possible to overcome such distortions by taking as a reference "the *regulative ideal* of an unrestricted and unconstrained communication."[18] As a consequence, a critique of ideology is informed by an orientation to the future and is sustained by the promise of an eventual emancipation from the repressive effects of power and its application. But it is also this hopeful outlook that signals the main weakness of the Habermasian approach. For Ricoeur, this eschatological view of freedom fails to take into account the weight traditional sources of communicative action exert on any conceptualization of future possibilities. The view is therefore vulnerable to a hermeneutical critique. Ricoeur points out that an interest in emancipation—which Habermas also refers to as "self-reflection"—has to be grounded somewhere: "For in the end, hermeneutics will say, from where do you speak when you appeal to *Selbstreflexion*, if it is not from the place that you yourself have denounced as a non-place, the non-place of the transcendent subject?" If recourse to the transcendent insight of an individual consciousness is unavailable, the alternative is to recognize that any project for emancipation has to be elaborated on the basis of a whole tradition of emancipation. In this regard, a "hermeneutics of tradition" offers a useful corrective and can serve to "remind the critique of ideology that man can project his emancipation and anticipate an unlimited and unconstrained communication only on the basis of the creative reinterpretation of cultural heritage."[19]

A more recent version of Ricoeur's analysis is to be found in the work of Charles E. Scott, who finds a similar conjunction of the traditional and the creative in the work of Nietzsche, Heidegger, and Foucault. Scott proposes that the originality of these thinkers is to be located in the creative manner in which they use tradition to open up new possibilities for thought: "They all find the possibility for their own thought in their philosophical heritage and take their departures from the suppression or avoidance that traditionally accompanies it."[20] Specifically, it is by engaging in a maneuver Scott calls a "self-overcoming recoil" that the three philosophers succeed in first making explicit whatever has been avoided or suppressed in the tradition and, second, in elaborating a thought that no longer needs to rehearse the traditional metaphysical patterns and ideas. Not only does such a discourse have the virtue of curing us of our illusions about comprehending or controlling reality, it also avoids the self-delusion of a critique of ideology, because "the curative aspect is not found in an illumination of a false discourse by a true one, but in a knowledge that finds itself both repeating and departing from the inheritances that it describes."[21]

It is also the conjuncture of repetition and departure that can be seen to mark the postmodern condition of the hermeneutical enterprise today. As Ormiston and Schrift explain,

> to refer to the "postmodernity" of interpretation is to refer to the possibilities of hermeneutics, the possibilities of histories and traditions, the possibilities of interpretation. As such, these possibilities, this condition, is "always already there"—that is to say, it is always already a *current issue* never limited in its effects to a specific historical moment. Passing from hand to hand, as it were, the word "interpretation" always circulates— suspending, fragmenting, decentering, but always transforming its object and subject in the experience of interpretation. The postmodernity of interpretation, then, indicates the ever-present possibilities of otherness, the difference(s) of sign and its object, of interpretation and the text that make the life of interpretation.[22]

Because the postmodern stance of interpretation is also predicated on the impossibility of imposing closure on the hermeneutical process, contemporary practice is marked by a sometimes explicit, sometimes unavowed suppression of the desire to reach definitive forms of knowledge and stages of knowing.

The resistance to the seducing prospects of true knowledge manifests itself in a variety of guises. Michel Foucault, for example, finds that techniques of interpretation have usually given rise to two main suspicions regarding language: one is "the suspicion that language does not say exactly what it means" and the other is "that in some way it overflows its properly verbal form."[23] Julia Kristeva discusses the political implications in the act of interpretation and proposes a psychoanalytic approach as an antidote to political discourse, especially in cases of "political delirium in avant-garde writing."[24] Jean-Luc Nancy explores examples of "the modern misinterpretation of interpretation."[25] The art of hermeneutics thus turns into a strategy for resisting the love of wisdom or *philosophia*. But it is also—and paradoxically—this strategic move that turns hermeneutics toward philosophy and makes interpretation seek a philosophical definition.

This paradoxical appropriation of philosophy by hermeneutics can also be seen as a symptom of the crisis besetting philosophy today. The philosophers who are interested in discerning the causes and the consequences of this crisis do not find in it a reason to despair, however. They generally regard it as the sign of a positive or encouraging turn of events in the history of Western thought because it has provided philosophy with the opportunity to reorient itself, to make itself self-critical—in short, to become hermeneutically more responsive and responsible.

One direction in which this reorientation has taken philosophy is fundamentally ethical in its emphasis. The work of Emmanuel Levinas has been particularly important in this regard; it exemplifies a tendency to invert the traditional way of thinking about the subject by bringing out the physical presence of others. Specifically, it is the "face" of the other that imposes itself as an ethical awareness: "The other person, from the first and prior to the constitution of meaning puts the self into a posture of debt that can best be characterized in terms of ethical debt, obligation to the other."[26] According to Levinas, the awareness of the other's presence with its concomitant recognition of moral responsibility are obvious aspects of our existence that have been neglected to a surprising extent in the history of Greek and European thought. Of course, if we take into account the importance given to the subject in this tradition, the neglect is readily understandable because, as Levinas shows, the presence of the other dispossesses the subject of its preeminent status: specifically, the other's "face" is the foil that resists all attempts at recuperation, understanding, and definition. This physical manifestation of the other "cannot be brought to full intuitive presence and this precisely because the 'presence' of the other person overwhelms subjectivity, overloads the subject, burdens the ego with more than its own abilities, more than its own active and passive syntheses can handle."[27]

Another important consequence of Levinas's insight is the awareness that being overwhelms language; otherness, therefore, is not accessible in language and "no individual, not even the most empty or stupid one, can be reduced to his or her work as if he or she were an event of language."[28] Understanding can no longer be attempted on the basis of an ideal of comprehension that takes a subjective consciousness as a starting point and assumes a language as the adequate means; as Richard Cohen points out, the presence of the other frustrates our attempts to recover it phenomenologically because "it occurs in an elicitation rather than an elucidation."[29] By granting the dative priority over the nominative, Levinas brings about a dual achievement. The subject is made to lose control over language and language, in turn, is shown to be inseparable from being. The empirical and transcendental find themselves inextricably commingled and, as a result, "all discourses must result in the undoing of the tissue they wove."[30] To explain further this particular nature of discursive activity, Levinas uses the logically absurd notion of the *anterior posteriori*. According to Levinas, any representation of reality is made possible by a capacity for representing that is already available, a representation that is "already implanted"; consequently, "the represented, the present, as a *fact*, already belongs to the past prior to its representation." Which means that "the a priori constitution of the object as performed by the idealist subject takes place only after the event, that is to say, a posteriori."[31] What is affirmed, Cohen notes, is that which is irreducible to discourse, or life itself. It is the manner of living life, or ethical necessity, that takes precedence over the discursive determination of meaning or epistemological necessity.[32]

It is important to note that the awareness of a subject's unavoidable dependence on an alterity that precedes and dominates it does not lead a hermeneutic approach to posit humanistic explanatory schemes but only to intensify the activity of interpretation. Derrida recognizes, for example, that the other manifests itself as *Anspruch*, as a convocation or demand addressed to us "from a space that is not contiguous with our own." Therefore, "to accept that the other precedes as a command or imperative would be to see that there is no *naming* of the other, no signing the signature of the other, without the recognition of the other's alterity and unnameability."[33] To accept this impossibility is also to accept the necessity to return to the text and "to its author through our reading of it in such a way that we recognize his or her *irreducible particularity*." Once more, such an approach involves "a sense of ethical responsibility which has to do with the particular, which is an *affirmation* of the particular over the universal."[34]

The emphasis on the particular provides an effective way of deconstructing what could be called the "natural attitude" of a commonsensical understanding, which can also be seen as a tactic for suppressing difference, as a "resistance to recognizing the Otherness of the Other."[35] At the same time, this invalidation of the commonsensical allegation of its own universality need not have recourse to a transcendent alibi: it is not philosophy that will transcend culturally imposed limits of rationality, "any transcendence will only be the accomplishment of social practices themselves."[36] We need only to look to other cultures to find examples of thinking that is free of the trammels that make us take our own Western mind-set for an absolute component of human nature, to discover that the reason we posit as the basis for our spirituality and humanity is but a "metaphysics of that which glorifies the 'I think.'"[37] Thus, for example, for Aboriginal people, "identity is not a self-possession but is the identity of the totem, an essence that fundamentally belongs to others."[38] Likewise, the ethical perspective of Tibetans rejects the idea of an autonomous self as a common form of self-delusion; for them, "the concept I is a way of viewing the world, or rather a way of being in the world, but it is not an entity that really exists."[39]

At the same time, as Kenneth Liberman points out, it is inconceivable that we could abandon a rationality that has provided a foundation for our society since the time of the Greeks. What we can do with the help of hermeneutical thinking is find ways of thinking this rationality that will make it less self-centered and less self-assured. Hermeneutics, in this sense, can create "a new path, a way out of and beyond transcendental discourses that force us to assume the primacy of agency and the ahistoricity of human subjects."[40] One such path, David Gruber argues, has been opened up by Foucault's genealogical approach, because "the function of a genealogical investigation into the emergence of the subject is to recover that which theory tends to forget about itself."[41] The forgetting is reinforced by themes of naturalness, timelessness, and ahistorical truths—in other words, by whatever our grammar and our history make us accept as true. Foucault's reconceptualization of power provides a striking example of the reversal his thinking effectuates in traditional approaches. McWhorter shows that "within the discourses of Western political theory—liberalism, Marxism, radicalisms of various sorts—thinking power typically means thinking some already constituted subjectivity who owns or holds and employs this machine or tool called power. . . . Thinking power in these discourses already entails the thought of a subjectivity originally exterior to power." By showing that "power is not to be thought as prior to and separable from events," that "power is to be thought as immanent in events," Foucault succeeds in discrediting "the dangerous notion of cause and separable effect."[42] The notion is dangerous because it has served to hide the actual workings of power and conveniently to impose domination in the name of higher principles.

In this regard, seen as a strategy for disclosing tactics that have operated behind alibis of a hackneyed and convenient morality, hermeneutical thinking can become a form of consciousness raising that is also able to overcome the limits of conventional rationales: "What is liberating about consciousness raising is the process by which one comes to understand one's situation and the reasons for it in ways that were previously unavailable."[43] This is particularly evident in the case of feminist criticism. For feminists, the purpose of a critique is to problematize a relation it maintains with a traditional discourse of philosophy. While a feminist discourse frequently employs the tools made available by a critical tradition, "despite this affinity between philosophical and feminist practice, insofar as one is a feminist, one also stands in a problematic relationship to the history of philosophy, precisely because it is the history of one's own subjugation, as well as the discourse that has provided many of the grounds and justifications for that subjugation."[44] This realization has produced a strategy of reading the canonical texts "against the grain," "in order to reveal gaps and lacunae, which leave room for an interventionist activity of rewriting that introduces a feminist voice which the logic of the text is powerless to control."[45]

Such a rereading of texts that causes them to deconstruct themselves can also be considered as a defining aspect of the postmodern attitude. The strategy partakes of a paradox that can be traced all the way back to the Greeks, because we can already detect in Aristotle's writing a dual role "both founding the effective history of metaphysics and harboring the critical seeds for the overcoming of metaphysics."[46] The example of Aristotle thus serves to illustrate Lyotard's fundamental insight that "the modern is always and already *post*, it bears the postmodern; in its nascent state, the post is always and already *modern*."[47] The insight has two important consequences. On the one hand, it reminds us that it is impossible to escape, transcend, obviate the conditions that give our knowledge its shape, since the language we would use to provide the escape is formed on the basis of that very knowledge. On the other hand, we also see that the conditions determining our knowledge are no longer what we think they are, even as we speak of them, and that the rules we think we must obey are always already obsolescent; consequently, "for Lyotard the postmodern presents the necessity of recognizing that in whatever domain, whatever field of inquiry, in whatever phrasic network, one is without a rule, one already judges without criteria."[48] Or, rather, one judges according to criteria that will be defined a posteriori, because the a priori determining the rules will become available to consciousness once it has become irrelevant: the time of our thinking is the future perfect. It is the pragmatic context of our activities that is always already rearticulating the rules according to which we must produce and transmit meaning; thus, "though the postmodern does not entail an abandonment or a forgetting of the modern (project), it does entail a destruction and 'liquidation' of the modern domain. But this happens from *within* the modern: the postmodern (condition) is 'undoubtedly part of the modern' as its *différend*."[49]

The aim of postmodern hermeneutical strategies is thus to exacerbate the discord at the heart of modernity, to reinforce those elements in modernity's discourse that hold the greatest promise for contesting its validity. Foucault's tactic, for example, is to exploit the fundamentally historical nature of knowledge: "*Historicity* in Foucault's discourse means movements-of-differing-from, plays of valences straying from their origins and even sometimes perhaps perverting, distorting, or destroying the conditions that gave them birth."[50] It is also this very tactic that has elicited accusations of betrayal and abdication from those still holding to a modernist ethos of intellectual activism and responsibility. The attacks of Habermas against an alleged French "neoconservatism" are perhaps the best known instance of the campaign to discredit postmodernism: "Habermas understands the relation between his own neo-Enlightenment project and the Heideggerian and Derridean postmodern discourses as a relation between a contemporary theory of rationality that takes political problems seriously and a postmodern discourse that has perversely given up any attempt to bring the resources of philosophy to bear on political issues."[51] Yet Habermas's own position is a highly vulnerable one, as we have already seen. It fails to account for the weight of tradition as well as for the pull of its own political and cultural predispositions on its eschatological projections. In addition, it assumes a cause-effect connection between philosophy and politics that is yet to be demonstrated; it is to be noted, therefore, that "this criticism of the postmodern *dissolution* of the bond between modern rationality and societal modernization depends, of course, upon the assumption that the bond is real."[52] Ironically, the methodological assumptions of ideology critique seem to coincide, at this juncture, with those of conservative critics of theory. Clearly, it is just as naive to hold philosophers responsible for guaranteeing the progress of humanity as it is to blame them for an alleged disintegration of civilized standards: "Derrida did not invent the decentering of the self, the self is already in the process of being decentered. Derrida, Levinas, Heidegger, and others are only chroniclers; their power rests only in a capacity to focus public attention. Philosophy follows history."[53]

It is because philosophy can no longer claim a transcendence that would place it above and outside history that it is inclined, today, to adopt a hermeneutical outlook. Conversely, hermeneutics also gains from this association with philosophy. As Gadamer notes, the notion of understanding finds itself promoted today to the very center of philosophical concerns because it is what "constitutes the fundamental structure of human existence."[54] It is this universal aspect of understanding that Jean Grondin wishes to illustrate as he outlines the history of hermeneutics. Grondin proceeds by drawing a sharp distinction between two trends—one that has sought to develop a rigorous method of interpretation, a veritable *Kunstlehre des Verstehens* (a "scientific art" of understanding), the other aiming to establish the validity of hermeneutics on its own terms.

The search for this newer art of interpretation derives from a fundamental dissatisfaction with existing explanatory schemes and can therefore be seen as yet another symptom of the currently experienced cultural and philosophical crisis. This crisis has had a profound impact on our understanding of processes of signification in particular and manifests itself mainly as the dissolution of connections that used to bind signs to their referents and words to things. It has given rise to a conceptual awareness of differing and deferring that also constitutes the core of the hermeneutical experience today, according to Grondin. At the same time, Grondin insists that a hermeneutical strategy cannot limit itself to this Derridean topos but has to realize that it is driven by another dissatisfaction—by the suspicion, already identified by Foucault, that there is always, in language, something more than language seeking to express itself, that "behind, no, 'within' language, there is always a *vouloir-dire* that goes beyond the limited order of perceptible sounds and signs."[55] This will to signify is not simply linguistic then, but is to be located at the point where language links up with life. Consequently, interpretation involves more than a method for deciphering word games: "Comprehension is not a method, but a form of life those who understand each other have in common."[56]

These insights present Grondin with a twofold task. On the one hand, he seeks to find out why the obsession with method took over the development of Western thought and eclipsed less intransigent models for interpretation. On the other, he wishes to valorize precisely those approaches that were suppressed by attempts to turn hermeneutics into a technique aspiring to scientific objectivity. In carrying out this dual strategy, Grondin is clearly influenced by Gadamer's procedure. Thus, he finds it highly significant that Gadamer's starting point in *Truth and Method* is a discussion of a speech given in 1862 by Helmholtz, the vice-rector of the university of Heidelberg. The purpose of the speech was to draw a fundamental distinction between the natural and the human sciences and its effect was to initiate a debate that has yet to be settled and that was to have a long-lasting effect on the development of such fundamental notions as truth and reality in Western culture. Grondin points out that, by singling out Helmholtz's speech, Gadamer is able to skip all "epistemological debates on the methodological specificity of the human sciences that preoccupied, starting with the end of the nineteenth century, such authors as Droysen, Dilthey, Misch, Rothacker, Weber, Windelband, Rickert and many others."[57]

Instead of wasting his time with a debate that turns out to be largely pointless, Gadamer is able to launch an attack against the neo-Kantian and positivist *idée fixe* that has made the human sciences answerable to an ideal of scientific objectivity. Gadamer's campaign, Grondin shows, is largely influenced by one of the earliest sources of hermeneutical thinking—an Augustinian insight according to which meaning transmitted by language "is not the logical meaning of the statement [*énoncé*] to be derived by means of abstraction but the whole of the constellation enacted by the statement."[58] Because the subsequent evolution of hermeneutics lost sight of this dimension, its history can be seen as a gradual impoverishment of the legacy handed down from Greek and Roman antiquity; thus, "the fixation of Western thought on the statement (logic) amounts to amputating language of its most essential dimension, which is the inscription of all discourse in a dialogue that precedes it as much as it surpasses it."[59] For Gadamer, one of the most evident causes for this impoverishment is the influence of Kant, which, by aestheticizing and subjectifying such principles as taste and judgment, discredited their cognitive dimension and "signed the death warrant of the humanist legacy."[60] Kant's influence also opened the door to the undertakings of such methologists as Wilhelm Dilthey, Emilio Betty, and E. D. Hirsch, theoreticians whose aim was to "impose rigorous canons on the exercise of interpretation in the human sciences."[61]

To counteract the influence of the objectivists, Grondin valorizes projects designed to reestablish the philosophical validity of hermeneutics. Their principal merit, Grondin shows, has been to enact a radical reversal that proposes misunderstanding rather than intelligibility as the starting point for interpretation. Such a project was initiated already by Schleiermacher but was to find its fullest elaboration in the work of Heidegger. For Heidegger, the starting point for a hermeneutical strategy was not interpretation of data or a text presented to an already informed consciousness but the interpretation of the very project to interpret. He therefore proposed that "interpretation will simply consist in elaborating or elucidating after the fact the situation of comprehension."[62] The purpose, as we have already seen, is no longer to escape the circularity of the process but to accept it for what it is, to see comprehension as an act of participation in a tradition, as an intention to enter into an ongoing dialogue. The truth to be sought is no longer to be related either to an origin or a telos but is to be recognized as hermeneutic in nature: questions of truth no longer concern the logic of statements but the question of being in all of its linguistic, psychic, and material implications.

Arguably, it is the recognition of these implications that gives the practice of hermeneutics its postmodern outlook and lucidity. While it accepts the responsibility of self-reflexion and self-explanation it also understands the process of developing understanding to be interminable. To claim understanding, as both Schlegel and Schleiermacher realized, is to be deluded about the fundamental incomprehension marking the existence of a finite subject: "To understand, is therefore to miss the specificity of the other, its irreducibility to myself."[63] The hermeneutical self-awareness of the subject makes it accept its participation in culture and society as an existence overseen by a discursive regime whose systematicity is beyond its control or comprehension. Hermeneutic lucidity makes the subject recognize this regime as a system fully implicated in the intangible determinants of history as well as those of being, a system "whose permutations are limited only by the pragmatics of context and desire."[64]

History, according to Grondin, is nothing more than the story of humanity's growing self-awareness. There are evidently moments in the evolution of humankind when this questioning becomes particularly intense and absorbing, when the question of the present and its meaning imposes itself with a particular urgency. The postmodern awareness is very likely a symptom of such a historical juncture. It can be seen as a response to the currently perceived need to explore the significance of the present moment in the evolution of our civilization, to search out manifestations of the trends and transformations taking place in the present configuration of cultural, social, political, and economic forces. As we try to reintegrate our experience within the realm of sense and understanding, we are, in effect, transforming the latter. Imperceptibly, our consciousness undergoes a reorganization, shifts take place in our sensibilities and our sensitivities; these, in turn, have an effect on our discursive formations and our practices. This does not mean the postmodern strategy aims to reintegrate everything within the bounds of some new system of rationality. It simply allows the rational to display its insufficiency and inefficiency by acknowledging all that which, by definition, falls outside its boundaries.

As Kierkegaard observed, "We live forward but understand backward." Postmodernity has lost the confidence modernity once had to actively prepare the future, to foretell and to foreordain what is to come. The postmodern strategy strives mainly to make sense of the present, to elucidate our current situation of comprehension. It helps bring out the contingent nature of the sense and the norms our cultural unconscious imposes on our understanding of our world. A postmodernist critique of our cultural imaginary thus helps provide new possibilities for questioning and demythifying the established moral and cognitive orders by revealing the specific, selfish interests these orders serve under the cover of universal and eternal verities.

3

MICHÈLE LE DOEUFF'S
PHILOSOPHY OF DISINVOLVEMENT

What makes Michèle Le Doeuff's philosophical project especially compelling at this stage of modernity's waning is the intimate yet problematic connection she posits between her thought and herself as a woman. It is a link that both stimulates and troubles her; as she explains, "I am woman, philosophy is my trade, chosen partly because I am a woman, and yet there is a tension between these two things." And she adds, "Let us set this tension to work." The source of Le Doeuff's critical strategy is thus to be located in an acute awareness of what she identifies as her own inescapably paradoxical theoretico-subjective position. She describes herself as a *femme-philosophe-féministe*, explaining that, "when you are a woman and a philosopher, it is useful to be a feminist in order to understand what is happening to you" (28). Her feminist standpoint is then the intellectual framework allowing her to exploit critically her tense relationship with philosophy, a discipline she finds alternately repulsive and alluring—as any woman would, she believes.

It is with this ambivalence in mind that she dedicates the volume of essays entitled *Hipparchia's Choice* (*L'étude et le rouet* in French) to "those young women preparing to enter a world where it will be held against them that they do not belong to the side of the Almighty, and thus that they believe and spread the belief that intelligence lies elsewhere."[1] In Le Doeuff's experience, two things are undeniable about philosophy. On the one hand, it is essentially sexist; on the other, it has also been her path to freedom. Her response to this dilemma is eminently logical—intelligence is not where it pretends to be and thus has to reside somewhere else.

Instead of trying to reach some form of accommodation with the icons of philosophical tradition who posit women's intellectual inferiority as a given, Le Doeuff simply declares that their thinking is fundamentally flawed and proceeds to "analyse stupid utterances made about women by people who, in principle, have no right to stupidity." She does this in order to show that such utterances "usually betray a theoretical weakness, a difficulty that the philosopher has been unable to overcome," and, consequently, that their real significance lies elsewhere (13).

Le Doeuff's critical strategy derives thus from two refusals. First, as a woman, she resists any intimation to feel inadequate in an intellectual realm thoroughly dominated by men. Second, while she distinctly feels alienated from a traditional form of philosophical discourse, she refuses to entertain any thought of giving up philosophy. She explains: "When I feel the difficulty of grasping and conceptualizing the 'woman question,' the question of women both in general and in philosophy, I have to conclude that this question cannot be integrated into our received frameworks of thinking, be it everyday thinking or that developed by philosophy. Such considerations lead me to wonder if all thinking might not be built on the rejection of a certain number of realities, of which that is one"(7). For Le Doeuff, it is evident that the deficiency attributed to women's intellect by such eminent figures as Aristotle, Kant, Hegel, and Comte is much more a reflection of a glitch in a given philosopher's brain than a sign of inadequacy on the part of women. The flaw is already apparent in the conventional assumption that a philosopher's activity consists of examining the objects of his inquiry in the light of a reason claiming universal validity and application. Such a stance is pure pretense, Le Doeuff shows, because it is, at bottom, nonsensical: "Philosophical universalism is this entirely assumed independence of the object of the debate in relation to the particular people who are debating it" (41). The philosopher assumes he can ignore his own subjective involvement with his project but he ignores the assumption's strategic implications. This obliviousness is of particular interest to women because the philosopher's conceit of a self-sufficient and superior stance is achieved at the expense of women; thus, "in the writings of a man philosopher, 'woman' may be no more nor less than a word for a foil whose role is to guarantee the philosopher's 'greatness' by contrast." As a consequence, concludes Le Doeuff, "sexism underpins the very method by which a system of thought is established" (xi–xii).

Yet it is also pointless to delve into what philosophers have said about women; what is important is to understand the way in which these assertions function within their overall theoretical scheme of explanations. That is why Le Doeuff wishes to study "not the misogynist stupidities that appear in philosophical texts, but the gap between these howlers and the theoretical rigour required of the discourse in which they appear" (35). Le Doeuff's intellectual chutzpah thus effectuates a reversal that brings about two notable results. First, she successfully turns the argument of male superiority against its promoters pointing out that "far from giving way to disgust, women should know that the sexism of philosophical discourse offers them a hold on that discourse" (14). Second, Le Doeuff's strategy produces some very revealing insights into the cultural and political importance of philosophical discourse.

It is thus by theorizing her own ambivalence toward philosophy that Le Doeuff uncovers the basic flaws characterizing philosophical systems. By revealing the subterfuges on which they are founded, she dismantles the pretentiousness of their claims. One such claim is that of "philosophic rigor." To bring out the delusion behind any assertion of "rigor," Le Doeuff demonstrates the unbreakable links between philosophy and everyday thinking—a connection that is evident to her as a woman. As a result, the philosophical problem is displaced from a consideration of philosophy in terms of the "great issues" to a question of philosophy's implication in the daily existence of people; thus, she asks, "what does the belief that there is a contradiction between being a woman and being a philosopher say about how women in general are thought of and what philosophy itself is thought to be?" (27) Le Doeuff's approach is therefore essentially hermeneutical in a Gadamerian sense, since she construes philosophy, not as a primary and original system standing on its self-generated apodictic evidence but as a system built on a tacit incorporation of common prejudices characteristic of a culture and an age. What philosophers fail to realize, she shows, is that "in philosophical work essential values come first, before even thought itself. A set of values, which are simply assumed, structures the theoretical enterprise, providing at the least its governing rules and its meaning." As a result, any work of philosophy is always already structured by a "deep axiology." Unbeknownst to the philosopher, received ideas make their way into his work and predetermine from the outset its aims and thrust. The more the philosopher asserts his independence from the world of everyday thought, the more the flaw becomes evident. Thus, "any project describing itself as a simple exercise of clarification of burning issues is in fact coloured by values which the author keeps out of the discussion" (32).

According to Le Doeuff, all knowledges, all systematic attempts at explaining the world are erected on some fundamental misunderstanding; they are made possible by the rejection or occlusion of certain aspects of reality that prove too cumbersome, too awkward to be assimilated within the system. There exists then an area of *nonsavoir* in any intellectual endeavor, a space that is, at the same time, the point of its greatest weakness. To cover up this debilitating flaw, discursive strategies rely on the imaginary's powers of conviction and their capacity for covering up gaps in logic or common sense. One common instance of this stratagem is a reliance on images to sustain the force of an argument. For Le Doeuff, images become "the place of theory's impossible" because they tend to arise at junctures where the logic of an argument fails. Yet, while images are used to resolve theoretical difficulties, they are never acknowledged as something crucial to the argument: they are presented as simple rhetorical devices allowed to stand in an extrinsic, decorative relation to the issue at hand. Images are therefore symptomatic of a fundamental flaw or lack in a theoretical argument and, on examination, their meaning proves incompatible with the discourse's principal claims or pretense. This deficiency makes them useful from a critical standpoint because they can serve to reveal the duplicity of a philosophical argument as well as the precise points where it fails.

One of the most telling examples of this tactic of self-delusion is to be found in the philosophy of Jean-Paul Sartre, which relies on an imaginary representation of woman for articulating some of its arguments: "If Sartre's existentialism can be defined as a theorization of a megalomania of the subject ('nothing outside us has decided what we are'), we can then state that the term 'woman' appears in a contradictory way at decisive points where this megalomania is established and then contained" (p. 86). Because Sartre's imaginary is motivated by a pervasive androcentrism, "anything which could not be given a theoretical foundation, but is necessary to make the system hold together and makes it possible to ground and reiterate the theory, is provided by sexism" (87).

Existentialism is definitely not a feminism, reminds us one of Le Doeuff's chapter subheadings. As she explains, Sartre's system belongs to those philosophies in which "positive humanity is defined by contrast, through the production of an imago called woman" (89). Such an imaginary production is the necessary support of Sartrean existentialism because "Sartre cannot think of himself, . . . cannot, alas, understand the humanity of man other than by postulating woman as a foil or as a protagonist, either annexed by conquest or used as a negative, terrifying figure" (88). That is why, Le Doeuff shows, "woman is always seen only as a body, and a sexed body" in Sartrean discourse (62). This is particularly evident in *L'être et le néant* where Sartre uses the example of a woman claiming to be frigid to develop his notion of bad faith. Sartre relies on a case study described by the Viennese psychiatrist Steckel, in which a woman's claim not to experience sexual pleasure is countered with the husband's assertion that "his wife has given objective signs of pleasure" (65). Sartre's conclusion: there are no frigid women, only women who deny their pleasure. That Sartre would automatically lend credence to the man's version of a sexual encounter not only reveals his sexist bias but also the incoherence of his thought: "Against all the general assumptions of his own doctrine, Sartre thus draws on an 'objectivity of the sign' (and the objectivity of an emotional state perceived by another person!) . . . There are no signs in the world, but women's bodies provide signs which are objective" (68). Even the language Sartre uses betrays his complete oblivion to the predispositions of his own imaginary; he writes, for example: "What must be the being of man if he is to be capable of bad faith? Take the example of a woman who . . ." (72). "I am not making this up," adds Le Doeuff.

The sexism manifest in *L'être et le néant* can properly be called philosophical, notes Le Doeuff, "because it is used to give a solid basis to a concept, that of 'bad faith'" (p. 64). Behind the high-minded pretense of existentialist philosophy, Le Doeuff discovers the dismally self-indulgent designs of a banal French machismo and is struck by a disquieting thought: "Might not the great echo which Sartre's philosophy found in the collective consciousness arise from the fact that, far from displacing the models of social relations, it recycled their subjective quintessence using language in which they were unrecognizable?" (195). Sartre's sexism is therefore more than philosophical—or, to be more accurate, not at all philosophical since it represents the recycling of a commonplace imaginary that functions to victimize women in society; as Le Doeuff points out, "a deep-seated attitude is betraying itself here, a frightening but commonplace stupidity both on the political and human planes" (65). It is an attitude that manifests itself in various ways but with one element that remains a constant, namely the phallocentric pretense to know what woman wants, to understand her desire better than she does herself. One of its most common guises, for example, is the urge to blame the victim in instances of rape or of domestic violence. And Le Doeuff wonders: "To what extent is the monopolistic violence which, in Sartre's work, is structured around the position of the writer, specific, in other words unconnected to other more common and less literary forms of violence, such as ordinary domestic violence?" (195) By incorporating the macho attitude in its system, existentialism becomes "a system which seeks the connivance of masculinist ideology each time a case needs to be made for something unthinkable" (88). To achieve credibility, to cover up gaps in logic, Sartre's system must rely heavily on the legitimating effects of a pervasive phallocentric mythology.

Because a philosophy such as existentialism can readily avail itself of the support of a reigning masculinist ideology it also serves to lend credence to certain male-oriented popular myths. Thus, Le Doeuff notes, philosophers have often "graciously provided and still provide the common ideology with themes or models representing the intellectual inferiority of women," and because their systems have "grounded in reason the vocations that social life assigns to us anyway," they have successfully contributed to keeping women in their socially and culturally assigned place. Sartre thus becomes a striking exemplar of the philosopher who claims to explain the world but does so in terms of phantasms he has internalized and then reproduces as original conceptual discoveries that serve to render the system coherent. Le Doeuff concludes: "At its imaginary level, Sartre's philosophy rests on his social experience as a man, a European and a philosophy teacher which, taken as a whole, is an unequivocal experience of domination" (75).[2]

What makes Sartre's bad philosophical faith particularly glaring is his relationship with Simone de Beauvoir. Le Doeuff writes: "Here we find a stereotype in philosophical liaisons. Since the days of Antiquity, women have been admitted into the field of philosophy chiefly when they took on the role of the loving admirer: we can call this the 'Heloise complex'" (59). While Le Doeuff admires de Beauvoir and is sympathetic to her dilemma, she cannot help being appalled by de Beauvoir's submissiveness and sums up the intellectual relationship of Sartre and de Beauvoir by noting that "the first became the century's most visible philosopher and the second a tremendously well-hidden philosopher" (139). At the same time, Le Doeuff's feminist stance allows her to measure the distance covered since the time of Beauvoir and, because she is able to recognize de Beauvoir's pioneering contribution to the cause of feminism, she can outline a feminist program of practical activism that takes into account the lessons learned and progress made since the time of *The Second Sex*.

There is a critical as well as a constructive side to Le Doeuff's program. On the critical side, Le Doeuff rejects traditional strategies of systematic theorizing because it has become evident, by now, that "no philosophy has ever provided a theoretical basis for everything or proved everything it assures, unless it be in appearance, and appearance has played more than one trick on theoretical work itself" (8). It is precisely when philosophers attempt to ground the product of their cogitation on an unshakable basis that it becomes prone to self-delusion. As a consequence, Le Doeuff opts for a radically different strategy: "I therefore prefer to start by playing a different game: that of abstention on the questions that are supposedly fundamental and whose answers nevertheless seem destined to remain forever imaginary" (11). Not that Le Doeuff underestimates the influence of the imaginary on her own thinking; it is because of this very awareness that she is careful to keep her approach feminist but not feminocentric. She realizes that "the 'female condition' is not just the 'female condition': it reveals social structures which also weigh heavily on some men, in some situations" (36). A feminism that thinks philosophically, notes Le Doeuff, necessarily concerns both men and women. What is more, feminist or women's studies partake of a universality that philosophies grounded on a "masculinist particularism" can no longer claim since their pretense has become transparent. As a mode of intellection, "masculinism" can only act as an intellectual block or as a cover-up.

She admits, at the same time, that hers is "a philosophy which strictly speaking does not exist" (11). What motivates her, then, is the simple desire for a certain kind of "philosophy which will allow men and women to come together in a common task . . . a simple desire for a community of both sexes and a search for the practical and theoretical conditions which might make it possible to fulfill that hope" (xii). Her aims remain both practical and modest and she describes what she practices as a "migrant rationality which never wants to understand itself absolutely" (51). In order to keep in mind what can realistically be accomplished at a given juncture, Le Doeuff finds useful the notion of "kenning," a term used in navigation and referring to the horizon that determines the limits of the sailor's field of vision at any particular moment. Such an awareness of the limits imposed on our ability to understand and perceive makes us attentive to the potential influence of the unknown and the always possible intervention of the unpredictable: "the kenning, because it is limited, may always focus on forms which are falling into disuse, so that one can never be absolutely sure where the danger, regression or new form of oppression is coming from" (315). Thus, she finds that "the kenning we need to give ourselves in politics is that of a generation" (303).

Le Doeuff's political strategy is thus distinctly pragmatic: what matters most, in many cases, is not changing people's minds—an interminable and unpredictable process at best—as changing numbers and ratios. She supposes, for example, that "if we could establish today that all authorities or decision-making bodies should be composed of equal numbers of men and women, sexism would very probably disappear from school textbooks" (303). If the reality changes, thinking will follow. Values are derived from the reality they reflect: they are meaningless by themselves and have little power to change reality. It is in this perspective that Le Doeuff determines a connection linking philosophy to politics. One of the traditional pretenses of philosophy has been to stand clear of any political involvement. Le Doeuff uses the notion of equality to demonstrate the insidious manner in which ideology permeates a philosophy that claims to be objective and disinterested. Equality, she argues, is a philosophical issue precisely because it is a political one: "Inequality between male and female individuals is an effect of the relationships they have with a third party, that being one or several authorities, which we should always try to uncover. The fact that one always finds the state in its relationship to 'delegated administration' enables us to politicize everything" (308). Consequently, everything that constitutes daily life, existence in its minutest details, "the tiny elements of relations between men and women or between institutions and people, can be seen as linked to politics" (255). The reasons for inequality or injustice may not be immediately apparent and "the 'cause' of a form of inequality, like that of a sexist mechanism, may be very distant" (308). To get at this cause, we need to question commonplace assumptions, received ideas, scrutinize beliefs, official pretexts and pretenses, analyze the thought surrounding institutionalized patterns of behavior; it becomes important, therefore, to clear away "the twaddle, even in its tiny trivial aspects" because, in so doing, "we can hope to be doing useful work. Assuming it is blocking our view, then overturning it means helping another generation to see further or to look elsewhere" (313).

Moreover, the dissatisfaction with commonly accepted truths and with received ideas is a most legitimate motive for undertaking a philosophical project. Philosophy, Le Doeuff argues, is always born of dissatisfaction, of the realization that "Some knowledges leave the mind unsatisfied, some intellectual food does not nourish, some theories block intelligence or screen out awareness of something which absolutely must be known" (213). It is also in this sense that the feminism exemplified by Le Doeuff's strategy can be situated at the very center of the philosophical strategies that guide today's critical reexamination of modernity and all of its Eurocentric, colonialist, and phallocentric derivatives. It is a feminism, moreover, that shares in the success of the critical strategies and cultural circumstances contributing to uncover the pretenses set in place at the dawn of the modern age.

One such pretense, as we have seen, is the masculine-feminine opposition that philosophy has helped to articulate and define. The strategic move to relegate women's thinking to a secondary status and to take it as the very proof that legitimates a metaphysics of masculine rationality has produced a reversal: what stands out today, in the context of today's philosophical and scientific discoveries on the subject of reason is the delusion and obtuseness of the principal defenders of male superiority in the domain of cogitation. Le Doeuff singles out three such figures. One is Jean-Jacques Rousseau, who found it evident that "the search for abstract and speculative truths, for principles and axioms in the sciences, for all that tends to wide generalizations is beyond the grasp of women; their studies should be thoroughly practical. . . . Woman should discover, so to speak, an experimental morality, man should reduce it to a system. Woman has more wit, man more genius; woman observes, man reasons."[3] Rousseau even proposes that woman's inadequacy in intellectual matters be construed as a significant component of her charm; the ingenuousness of such an argument can only reveal something fundamental about Rousseau's own intellect, suggests Le Doeuff: "'Oh lovely ignorance' says

Rousseau of the future 'man's woman.' To postulate and indeed love the principle of the other's ignorance always comes down to revealing or ignoring one's own stupidity" (51).

Another well-known promoter of the superiority of male reason was Hegel, who asserted that

> Women may be capable of education, but they are not made for the more advanced sciences, for philosophy and certain forms of artistic production which require universality. Women may have ideas, taste, and elegance, but they do not have the ideal. The difference between men and women is like that between animals and plants; men correspond to animals, while women correspond to plants because their life is more a placid unfolding, the principle of which is the undetermined unity of feeling. When women hold the helm of government, the state is at once in jeopardy, because women regulate their actions not by the demands of universality, but by arbitrary inclinations and opinions. Women are educated—who knows how?—as it were by breathing in ideas, by living rather than by acquiring knowledge, while man attains his position only by the conquest of thought and by much technical exertion.[4]

The third example of philosophical obtuseness is provided by Auguste Comte, who argues, similarly to Rousseau, that woman should accept man's domination for her own good:

> It is in order better to develop her moral superiority that woman must gratefully accept the rightful practical domination of man . . . First as a mother, and later as sister, then above all as a wife, finally as a daughter, and possibly as a maidservant: in these four natural roles woman is destined to preserve man from the corruption inherent in his practical and theoretical existence. Her affective superiority spontaneously confers on her this fundamental office, which social economy develops increasingly by releasing the loving sex from all disturbing cares, active or speculative.[5]

However one might wish to analyze the three texts quoted, what stands out, today, is the intellectual limitation founding all these philosophies, an ignorance going back to a fundamental error made by Descartes and subsequently enshrined by Kant, Hegel, and others. The authority of these foolish assertions is vested in a theoretical discourse legitimating clear-cut distinctions between mind and body, subject and object. This separation of the realms of intellect from soma is what allows the further discrimination between masculine and feminine modes of thought: on the one hand, it is taken as axiomatic that the female of the human species is incapable of maintaining the mental separate from the somatic, the emotional from the rational. The male, on the other hand, is given the capacity to dwell in the realm of pure thought and to see life in the light of an unadulterated rationality. Today, in the light of discoveries made in neuroscience, it turns out that such a state is principally enjoyed by victims of severe brain injuries or by mental patients who have undergone frontal lobotomies.

Specifically, and contrary to what Descartes propounded, it has become clear, as Antonio Damasio—a leading expert in the field of neurobiology—points out, that "mind" encompasses the entire body and "derives from the entire organism as an ensemble."[6] The mind is therefore seen as something constituted by the organism's interaction with the environment to which it is subject and with which it must contend—it is less an originator of understanding as its recipient, since it must function, at the most basic level, as a mechanism that ensures the organism's survival and well-being; consequently, it partakes of an evolutionary history that is both biological and cultural; being is primordial, thus, and Descartes' proposition finds itself inverted: according to Damasio, "We are, and then we think."

The title of Damasio's book—*Descartes' Error*—echoes a philosophical theme whose development marks the evolution of Western thought over the last two centuries. It reflects as well the consensus of the present, postmodern juncture in critical thinking by underlining the discredit into which the Cartesian model has fallen. We can no longer separate the physical from the mental as readily as Descartes once did since it is clear that our knowledge "is shaped by both the world with which we interact and by the biases inherent in our organism." Moreover, Damasio supposes, "it is a fair assumption that most so-called brain-caused actions being taken at this very moment in the world are not deliberated at all."[7]

The function designated by the word *mind* thus finds itself relegated to a dependent status. This is because the mind cannot function as an autonomous unit and scientific research is increasingly leading specialists to believe "that the body, as represented in the brain, may constitute the indispensable frame of reference for the neural processes that we experience as the mind; that our very organism rather than some absolute external reality is used as the ground reference for the constructions we make of the world around us and for the construction of the ever-present sense of subjectivity that is part and parcel of our experiences."[8] The body "marks" certain images from our experience and provides these markers as orienting devices in decision-making by establishing cumulative preferences and, in given situations, by highlighting certain options. These are somatic markers that "can bias cognitive processes in a covert manner and thus influence the reasoning and decision-making mode."[9] Furthermore, the marking takes place in the prefrontal sectors that are the seat of emotions since they "establish dispositional representations for certain combinations of things and events, in one's individual experience, according to the personal relevance of those things and events."[10] At the same time, these predispositions or biases are integrated within the context of the individual's social and cultural norms thus taking on the appearance of rationality. This device, as Damasio points out, has been made "rational relative" to social conventions and to morality: "The automated somatic-marker device of most of us lucky enough to have been reared in a relatively healthy culture has been accommodated by education to the standards of rationality of that culture. In spite of its roots in biological regulation, the device has been tuned to cultural prescriptions designed to ensure survival in a particular society."[11] That is why, explains Damasio, "the immune system, the hypothalmus, the ventromedial cortices, and the Bill of Rights have the same root cause."[12] The "high-reason" or commonsense view is therefore fundamentally deluded, and "the cool strategy advocated by Kant, among others, has far more to do with the way patients with prefrontal damage go about deciding than with how normals usually operate."[13]

The truly revolutionary aspect such a view brings to our understanding of the human mind is the inseparability of the mental from the physical. It is an understanding that leads us to appreciate the entire organism's implication in the sociocultural environment: "To understand in a satisfactory manner the brain that fabricates human mind and human behavior, it is necessary to take into account its social and cultural context."[14] It is also in this regard that these latest discoveries made in the study of the brain meet with certain philosophical approaches that have sought to elucidate the phenomenon of understanding as indissociable from the fact of existing. Traditionally, the thinking subject's situation of comprehension has been invisible, that is, taken for granted as the natural and ever-present background for our thinking and activities. For today's critical theorists, it is the situation of being that has acquired a primary importance.

4

THE DIALECTIC OF REASON

A good part of the impetus sustaining critiques of the Enlighten-ment over the past three or four decades can clearly be attrib-uted to Adorno's and Horkheimer's well-known essay on the dialectic of the Enlightenment. As Mitchell Dean points out, "The centrality of the problem of enlightenment in late-twentieth century social thought is undoubtedly largely due to this one key text of the Frankfurt School."[1] The validity of Adorno's and Horkheimer's thesis has been further reinforced by Michel Foucault, who noted an affinity in approaches that, in his words, "makes us brothers with the Frankfurt School."[2] Foucault's interest in the best-known work produced by the Frankfurt School was evidently related to the disquisition he had undertaken on Kant's famous question, "Was ist Aufklärung?" He linked the growing importance of the issues raised in the *Dialectic of Enlightenment* to a questioning that was to be taken as a most revealing sign of the times. Thus he supposed that "in France we have come to a time when precisely this problem of Aufklärung (which had been so important for German thought since Mendelssohn, Kant, passing through Hegel, Nietzsche, Husserl, the Frankfurt School, etc.) can be taken up again in a meaningful enough proximity with, let us say, the works of the Frankfurt School."[3]

To be sure, as Foucault himself admitted, this confluence of critical approaches was somewhat surprising and unexpected, because, historically, the critical reflection on the Enlightenment had followed divergent tracks in Germany and France. It is a divergence Vincent Descombes finds indicated by the very use of the term "Aufklärung." The difference, he notes, is not only due to the fact "that *Aufklärung* is the German word, but that the actual thing that the word refers to is part of Kant's heritage: namely, the

Lumières minus a revolution in one's own country."[4] What this means is that the French Revolution provides both a specific historical context and an ideological reference for considering the Enlightenment and its legacy. As Descombes points out further, "We in France do not reason within the perspective opened up by a modern *project*. Rather, our thinking is determined by what one might call a modern *accomplishment*. We do our thinking in the wake of our Revolution, the legacy of which deeply unites us even before dividing us from one another. And this can only mean one thing: *we reason in the wake of the (French) Revolution's failure to liberate humanity*." It is then the perception of a discrepancy—not the essence or reality of a concept—that becomes the motivation for the questioning, the question to be addressed from a French perspective being: "How does the collective system of representations that allows the French to identify themselves as *French citizens* reconcile itself to the obvious discrepancy between the revolutionary promise and the postrevolutionary experience?"[5] It is a discrepancy that can also be seen to underlie Foucault's approach to the question of the Enlightenment.

Foucault traces the German critical tradition culminating in Adorno's and Horkheimer's work back to Kant and, in particular, to the manner in which the latter construed critique as an essential component of the Aufklärung. Following Kant, notes Foucault, "This interrogation of the relations between Aufklärung and critique will legitimately take the demeanor of a distrustful, or in any case, of a more and more suspicious interrogation: for what excess of power, for what governmentalization (all the more ineluctable as it is justified in reason) is this reason itself historically responsible?"[6] It is a suspicion that became a particularly powerful critical motif in Germany where, Foucault tells us, "From the Hegelian Left to the Frankfurt School there was a whole critique of positivism, of objectivism, of rationalization, of *techné* and of technicization, a whole critique of the relations between the fundamental project of science and of technique that has as its objective making apparent the ties between a naive presumption of science, on the one hand, and the forms of domination proper to the form of contemporary society, on the other."[7] For Foucault, the history of this critical development entails two major considerations. He notes, first, that it is the kind of critique that could never have evolved in France because of the political importance the twin themes of Enlightenment and Revolution have had in sustaining the discourse concerning the Republican origins of the French State; he therefore supposes that "the bloc constituted by the Lumières and the Revolution no doubt hindered in a general way this relation of rationalization and power from being really and profoundly called into question."[8] Second, Foucault also notes that the Enlightenment, as it has been conceptualized in the German critical tradition, has become something entirely different from a French representation of *Les Lumières*. While the French approach has been to locate the Enlightenment within the boundaries of a specific historical period, in the German tradition the eighteenth century is but an especially vivid manifestation of a profound trend spanning nearly two and a half thousand years of Western civilization.

It is a perspective that becomes evident at the outset in Adorno's and Horkheimer's treatise. Accordingly, the eighteenth century is viewed as simply the culmination of a process inscribed in the sociopolitical destiny of the West. The notion of the dialectic serves both to explain and justify this perspective. That is, the dialectic serves a dual function—heuristic as well as critical: it is taken to characterize the very process through which we apprehend reality and, as a consequence, it is considered as the most effective critical approach to the knowledge we develop of reality. As David Held explains, it is an understanding that marks the thought of an eminent philosophical tradition, stretching from the ancient Greeks to the nineteenth century: "For Hegel, the dialectic is, as it had been for Plato, 'a cognitive power and a cognitive method, because . . . reality itself is dialectical.'"[9] Thought can only pretend to seize reality by means of concepts, thus "What distinguishes the dialectical method is the recognition of the insufficiencies and imperfection of 'finished' systems of thought. The dialectical method is a critical method for it reveals incompleteness where completeness is claimed."[10]

To remain effective then, a dialectic has to constantly negate itself—it has to recognize its own propensity to take itself too seriously as truth. For Adorno, a dialectic is negative by definition because it is "a critique of the fact that critique itself, contrary to its own tendency, must remain within the medium of the concept. . . . It lies in the definition of negative dialectics that it will not come to rest in itself, as if it were total. This is its form of hope."[11] Commonsensical uses of language and a belief in its representational capacity make us forget that talk of reality is derivative and that, in conscious thought as well as in discourse, access to reality is always/already mediated. Consequently, as Marcuse points out, to know what a thing really is, we have to "get beyond its immediately given state . . . and follow out the process in which it turns into something other than itself. . . . Its reality is the entire dynamic of its turning into something else and unifying itself with its 'other.' The dialectical pattern represents, and is thus 'the truth of,' a world permeated by negativity, a world in which everything is something other than it *really* is . . . , and in which opposition and contradiction constitute the laws of progress."[12]

The dialectical method's negative thrust thus aims to bring out the contradiction between concept and thing as well as the incompleteness of the process of reflecting and representing the real. What it succeeds in disclosing in this manner is the delusion perpetrated by a reliance on abstract thought. Abstraction is a constant source of illusion because it needs to posit a separation of subject and object in order to endow the subject with an "objective" capacity to constitute a knowledge of the real. Abstraction thus operates on the basis of a principle of immanence; it makes knowledge self-validating by denying the legitimacy of an outside or of an other in the process of knowledge acquisition. Abstract thinking creates a world in its own image by relying on the unimpeachable nature of the conceptual system it has created: "The concept, which some would see as the sign-unit for whatever is comprised under it, has from the beginning been instead the product of dialectical thinking in which everything is always that which it is, only because it becomes that which it is not."[13] In other words, the concept reifies otherness by imposing its logic on the world: everything is always that which it is when the world is assumed to be amenable to the simplifying logic of the conceptual realm. By establishing itself as a criterion of correct thinking the concept becomes that which it is not—reality itself. The procedure is therefore fundamentally tautological, as Adorno and Horkheimer explain it: "Factuality wins the day; cognition is restricted to its repetition; and thought becomes mere tautology. The more the machinery of thought subjects existence to itself, the more blind its resignation in reproducing existence. Hence enlightenment returns to mythology, which it never really knew how to elude" (27).

Enlightenment itself turns out to be no more than a pretense because of a blind spot that is inherent in its constitution. While Enlightenment gains its validity in combating myth, it fails to realize that myth is but its own creation: myth comes into being as the other of the positive, empirical, and logical kind of thinking Enlightenment presumes to sustain according to what it assumes are universal cognitive norms. At its most extreme, this kind of thinking has tended to espouse the form of a calculus: "Formal logic was the major school of unified science. It provided the Enlightenment thinkers with the schema of the calculability of the world . . . numbers became the canon of the Enlightenment" (7). Thus, as Adorno and Horkheimer see it, scientific or mathematical thinking become a major source of delusion: "Mathematical procedure became, so to speak, the ritual of thinking. In spite of the axiomatic self-restriction, it establishes itself as necessary and objective: it turns thought into a thing, an instrument—which is its own term for it" (25).

Moreover, according to Adorno and Horkheimer, the pattern for this tautological process is already apparent in the literature of the ancient Greeks: "The venerable cosmos of the meaningful Homeric world is shown to be the achievement of regulative reason, which destroys myth by virtue of the same rational order in which it reflects it" (44). They also credit Nietzsche with having been "one of the few after Hegel who recognized the dialectic of the enlightenment [and who] stressed the bourgeois enlightenment element in Homer" (44). This bourgeois element has attained its fullest realization in our modern, twentieth-century civilization, when the process involving the production and marketing of commodities has put in place a pattern of domination that ensures the perpetuation of bourgeois values; thus, "reason itself has become the mere instrument of the all-inclusive economic apparatus" (30).

As a result, because it has lost its capacity to develop a self-critical perspective, the Enlightenment has been coopted to serve as a cover for the socioeconomic process and has become, as Adorno and Horkheimer put it, "an ideological curtain behind which the real evil is concentrated" (xv). The system of mass production, commodification, and entertainment constitutes indeed a new kind of metaphysics since it is that which legitimates the social order. At the same time, we need to recognize that ever since the eighteenth century this order could not have been sustained without "the conventional attempt of bourgeois thought to ground respect, without which civilization cannot exist, upon something other than material interest and force" (85). Whence the need for the ideological alibi offered by the Enlightenment. Cast in the role of alibi, the Enlightenment becomes the instrument of the dominating class by serving the interests of various incarnations of the burgher to be found "in the successive forms of slave owner, free entrepreneur, and administrator" (83).

From Adorno's and Horkheimer's standpoint then, the critique of Western civilization is effectively carried out by locating the point at which politics and philosophy converge. This point is reason. By showing reason's propensity to serve the interests of the dominating order, they are able to argue that the Enlightenment, which was reason's most triumphant achievement, was doomed as soon as it took reason to be the immutable guarantor of its validity. Consequently, they see the Enlightenment as "a two-thousand-five-hundred-year development in Western civilization culminating in its ultimate perversion by bourgeois society" (85).

Paradoxically, but in keeping with the dialectical approach of their analysis, this pessimistic view also brings with it the corollary of a hopeful perspective. Domination can never be absolute since the very strategy that imposed it makes it vulnerable to an inevitable reversal: "In domination the aspect of rationality prevails as one that is also different from it. The 'objectivity' of the means, which makes it universally available, already implies the criticism of that domination as whose means thought arose" (37). As soon as thought appears as ideology, it loses its power to bind. As soon as it becomes clear that the means or rationale whereby reality is posited and order is imposed is actually heterogenous to this order and reality, the rationale's power to legislate and validate is brought into question, as are the status of reality and the legitimacy of a particular order. Reason has, in effect, been displaced. The reason that had served to establish domination is voided in the process and reappears as a critique that reveals "the rationality of the rational society as obsolete" (38–39). The most that can be said about reason then, is that it is pure movement, or function, but that it disintegrates as soon as it is brought to rest, as soon as it is conceptualized or represented.

It is this aspect of the German critical tradition that Foucault values in particular and considers to have had a lasting impact on the way we look at the legacy of the Enlightenment today. Summarizing the merits of this tradition, he observes: "That which was understood by Aufklärung . . . was certainly considered an important episode, a kind of vivid manifestation of the profound destiny of Western reason . . . In the Aufklärung and in this whole period—which, in short, from the sixteenth to the eighteenth century serves as a reference for this notion of Aufklärung—one tried to decipher, to recognize the most prominent line of ascent of Western reason, while it was the politics to which it was tied that became the object of a distrustful examination."[14] At the same time, Foucault's own approach to the question of the Enlightenment diverges fundamentally from that of the Frankfurt School. For Foucault, what matters is not the extent to which the Enlightenment fulfills or betrays an ideal concept of reason but the manner in which it has constituted a specific, historically bound rationality. Thus Mitchell Dean finds that, on the one hand, Adorno's and Horkheimer's arguments are clearly conducted in terms of "a normative conception of reason, of what reason ought to be like, of why existing forms of knowledge and thought are deficient in relation to a particular ideal of reason." On the other hand, Dean also notes that "the notion of reason that emerges in Foucault's work is not a normative but a performative one. It questions reason in its use, not as a norm by which various historical forms of reason can be evaluated."[15]

Foucault's particular view of reason is also characteristic of his general critical approach. In this sense, the difference between Foucault and the Frankfurt School is also reflected in the contrast between Foucault and Habermas. Unlike Habermas, notes David Hoy, "Foucault does not think that to undertake a rational critique of rationality one must either construct a theory of what rationality *really* is or fall into deep irrationality."[16] To define reason by opposing it to reason's other or to base one's investigations on some preestablished notion of reason is therefore considered futile. Also, in this regard, as Vincent Descombes reminds us, the opposition of reason to myth actually constitutes a false dialectic: "Myth is not the other of reason, it is merely another domain of human reason."[17] Similarly, for Foucault, "reason is self-created," that is, reason and norms of rationality evolve together with the project of making sense of the world and of themselves in which humans are constantly engaged. As Hoy tells us, "The point of Foucault's genealogical historiographies is not to destroy reason, but to remind us that reason's assumption of its own necessity and universality may be an illusion that ignores its historical formation in the past, its precariousness in the present, and its fragility in the future. Correlatively, genealogy analyzes practices that were instituted in the name of reason but that threaten to harden into unquestioned but oppressive necessity."[18]

Foucault's genealogical method is especially effective in its critical approach to the Enlightenment because it displays an affinity with a critical dilemma Patrick Madigan places at the very heart of the Enlightenment project. The strategy of the Enlightenment, argues Madigan, develops in terms of a critical reason that tends both to assert and question its autonomy. On the one hand, inspired by scientific advances and still imbued with the Cartesian spirit, the Enlightenment is an integral part of the "Modern Project to Rigor," an enterprise seeking to make reason into a reliable tool of inquiry and cognition. On the other hand, the Enlightenment also develops as a critical strategy valorizing its own autonomy. As a result, "the criticism which demonstrates, reinforces, and bolsters its confidence in freedom is also and at the same time the criticism which questions, opposes, and threatens to undermine it."[19] Unable to reconcile the opposing notions of freedom and determinism under the aegis of a uniform and unifying reason, the Enlightenment ends up oscillating between the two tendencies. It is a dilemma informing Foucault's own perspective, since he rejects the notion of a unitary reason. That is why one of the problems that concerns Foucault most, eventually, is the manner in which the nineteenth century will resolve this dilemma by way of an analytic of finitude—a self-centered and circular procedure that will take the very limitations of human cognition to be the legitimating marks of its accuracy and validity. The Enlightenment itself remained sufficiently lucid to resist this tendency to enclose itself in self-legitimation. It is a lucidity that comes at a cost, however, since it undermines the single-minded purposefulness an effective critique requires. As David Held sees it, it is also the unresolved dilemma of the Frankfurt School: "How can critical theory at once acknowledge its historicality and yet be critical? How can critical theory be part of the movement of history and a means of enlightenment?"[20]

The thesis put forward by the *Dialectic of Enlightenment* makes it therefore impossible to evade this quandary. As they consider the legacy of the Enlightenment, Adorno and Horkheimer, for their part, find everything to be subsumed under reason—even reason's self-betrayal. Foucault, on the other hand, is struck by the heterogeneity of the processes that are at work behind such vague abstractions as Reason or the Enlightenment. His approach, therefore, consists of elaborating a genealogy of whatever may have contributed to the formation of the rationalities sustaining these ontological motifs. This is why, suggests Dean, "The Foucaultian project is one of 'critical inquiry into the history of rationality,' or, if you like, a critical inquiry into the history of forms of practical reason and not an analytical of truth in the sense he ascribed to Kant, of discovering the universal principles of the legitimate use of reason."[21] Accordingly, the view that the Enlightenment is part and parcel of reason's destiny accounts for what Foucault calls a "slippage" in Kant's understanding of critique, a misconstrual that characterizes the subsequent evolution of a Kantian kind of critical approach in the nineteenth and twentieth centuries. For Foucault, "the essential function of critique would be that of desubjectification in the game of what one could call, in a word, the politics of truth."[22] The goal, then, is to deconstruct and disable the pretense, which is usually a reference to an essence or a universal motif serving to lend legitimacy or an air of truth to a discourse while helping to cover up the concrete and less noble self-serving interests of a discourse's political strategy.

What Foucault discovers is that his definition of critique is also the Kantian definition—not of critique, however, but of the Enlightenment. Critique, for Kant, consists of a questioning of the metaphysical grounds for critique, that is, of the transcendental motives establishing the validity of reason and of knowledge. As Foucault explains it, from a Kantian perspective, "critique will say, in sum, that our freedom rides less on what we undertake with more or less courage than in the idea we ourselves have of our knowledge and its limits."[23] Such an approach is misguided, from a Foucaultian perspective, because it favors the abstract over the particular, it discounts the everyday practical involvement with living and promotes a transcendental notion of reason as the essential backdrop for action; in short, it construes what is but a pretense into a fundamental support for thought. It is an approach that makes the critic lose sight of the concrete, historically bound circumstances attending the very formation of what one takes to be the unshakable basis for critique.

In short, Foucault proposes that critical priorities be inverted. If we begin with reason as a given, we immediately occlude the historicity of a particular way of thinking about a universal such as reason. Therefore, he asks, "Would one not now have to try to take the inverse path to this movement of tipping over, to this slippage, to this way of displacing the question of Aufklärung onto critique? Could one not try to take this path, but in the other direction?"[24] More specifically, as Foucault points out, it is "the very question of that event and its meaning (the question of the historicity of thinking about the *universal*) that must now be kept present in our minds as what must be thought."[25]

It is not the problem of reason that should bring up, as a corollary, the question of the Enlightenment, it is the question of the Enlightenment that should make us problematize the whole pretense of reason, that is, the very essence of modernity: "It is because one wants to pose fundamentally the problem 'Was ist Aufklärung?' that one encounters the historical scheme of our modernity. It will not be a matter of saying that the fifth-century Greeks are a little like eighteenth-century philosophers or that the twelfth century was already a kind of Renaissance, but rather of trying to see under what conditions, at the price of what modifications or what generalizations, one can apply to any moment of history this question of Aufklärung, the relationship of power, truth, and the subject."[26] This question is indeed *the* critical question from Foucault's perspective, since, for him, "the focus of critique is essentially the cluster of relations that bind the one to the other, or the one to the two others, power, truth, and the subject."[27] And it is by disconnecting the subject from the other two terms, by "desubjectifying" a discourse, that one uncovers the mechanisms of truth and knowledge that function in a given historical and sociopolitical setting.

Since reason is the subject of the Enlightenment, it is by disregarding rationality as a founding justification for the age or the civilization in question that the critic is able to pose the proper questions. One does not take rationality for granted and then develop a critique: one questions this very foundation: "How is this rationality born, how is it formed, from something that is wholly other? Here is the reciprocal and inverse of the problem of Aufklärung: How is it that rationalization leads to the rage of power?" What Foucault is suggesting is that an abstraction such as "rationality" never exists in and of itself, that manifestations of a "rationality" are tied to a whole field of conditions and determinants operating at a level that may not appear at all relevant to the formation and validation of knowledge. Foucault proposes, for example, that before anything can be accepted as legitimate "knowledge," it must conform to a whole system of requirements: "For nothing can appear as an element of knowledge if, on the one hand, it does not conform to an ensemble of rules and constraints characteristic, for example, of some kind of scientific discourse in a given epoch, and if, on the other, it is not endowed with effects of coercion or simply incitation proper to what is valid as scientific or simply rational or simply commonly received, and so on."[28] Rationality is thus reduced to a material level of "effects of coercion or incitation" proper to a given age and society: it is not seen as a natural or transcendental given but as a concrete strategy of promotion and selection. It is in this light that it becomes possible to effectively bring up "the question of the relations between the structures of rationality that articulate the true discourse and the mechanisms of subjugation that are tied to it."[29]

"Experience has taught me," observes Foucault, "that the history of various forms of rationality is sometimes more effective in unsettling our certitudes and dogmatism than is abstract criticism."[30] What makes abstract criticism ineffectual is that it is itself prone to developing the dogmatism of a priori certitudes because it will typically operate in terms of already established ontological principles. The circularity of such a critical approach makes it inherently judgmental: it unmasks untruths only to reveal the truth that served as the driving motive of its own will to critique. To escape dogmatism, it must turn against itself—but in doing so it ends up invalidating its own grounds: "Critique is condemned therefore to either a total critique cannibalizing itself or a dogmatism that asserts the a priori truth of the grounds on which it rests."[31] It is a dilemma, as Dean shows, that clearly affects the thesis of the *Dialectic of Enlightenment*. Foucault's approach avoids this dilemma because it does not assume a totalistic or judgmental relation to its object. Claiming no a priori ground for its inquiry, it is free to unmask untruths without having to uncover new truths.

By its refusal to base critique on an a priori judgment, Foucault's approach shows a marked affinity with the Nietzschean notion of the "Innocence of all Becoming." This presumption of *Die Unschuld des Werdens*, as Madigan explains, is "the doctrine which asserts that all forms or stages of existence (because determined and necessary) are of equal worth (or of equal nonworth). There are no standards of value."[32] It is in this sense, I believe, that we can appreciate Foucault's insistence on the necessity to discard the guidance of "philosophies of the subject." To understand history, including that of the Enlightenment, Foucault finds it necessary to forego all the founding themes that function to legitimate knowledge. The familiar categories of humanist thought and the methodology of a traditional history of ideas are to be shunned because "that which it is a matter of making stand out in order to grasp what could make them acceptable is precisely that which is not self-evident, it was inscribed in no a priori, it was contained in no anterior condition."

While some critics of Foucault have located the greatest weakness of his theorizing in his rejection of universals, it is precisely the evidence of the loss of credibility that universals have sustained in our century that motivates Foucault's approach. Adorno's and Horkheimer's dialectic view of the Enlightenment, while critical of Enlightenment's legacy, is still predicated on a continuity that is taken to be the inherent mark of Western thought. Foucault's approach posits a break between our time and the onset of modernity. Thus, the effectiveness of a Foucaultian critique can be attributed to the realization that the thought marking our time operates according to a scheme that no longer corresponds to whatever went under the designation of the Enlightenment. Our thinking, in this regard, is faced with a difficulty that turns out to be an integral part of the Enlightenment's legacy. Therefore, Foucault tells us, "I think that the central issue of philosophy and critical thought since the eighteenth century has always been, still is and will, I hope, remain the question: *What* is this reason we use? What are its historical effects? What are its limits, and what are its dangers?"[33] It is a question that provides the principal focus for Foucault's critique of the Enlightenment.

5

Foucault's Critique
of the Enlightenment

While Foucault's approach to the question of the Enlightenment can be said to avoid the dilemma affecting Adorno's and Horkheimer's thesis, it is still subject to a seemingly intractable paradox. On the one hand, as we have seen, its purpose is to avoid the limitations of a ground or subject that will prejudge the object of inquiry. On the other hand, it does not claim autonomy or the freedom of a superior vantage but accepts that it is itself implicated in whatever it seeks to elucidate or explain. In this sense, it appears to be guided by a hermeneutical insight formulated by Gadamer, namely that "we understand texts that have been handed down to us on the basis of expectations of meaning which are drawn from our anterior relation to the subject."[1] But it is also the realization that this anterior relation to the subject of investigation can itself be investigated that leads Foucault to effectuate a crucial reversal. It is a move made explicit with regard to Kant's approach to the question of the Enlightenment. Foucault explains: "If the Kantian question was that of knowing what limits knowledge has to renounce transgressing, it seems to me that the critical question today must be turned back into a positive one: in what is given to us as universal, necessary, obligatory, what place is occupied by whatever is singular, contingent, and the product of arbitrary constraints?"[2] It is a diplomatic way of suggesting that perhaps there is really nothing much at all that is preordained. Thus the necessity to recognize that what appears natural or ingrained in our ways of thinking could very well be fortuitous and not related to either the meaning of our being or of our collective destiny.

As he brings up the question of the Enlightenment's historical origins and reflects on the applicability of Kant's question to our own time, Foucault finds that criticism has necessarily changed: "Criticism is no longer going to be practiced in the search for formal structures with universal value, but rather as a historical investigation into the events that have led us to constitute ourselves and to recognize ourselves as subjects of what we are doing, thinking, saying."[3] It is this approach that allows Foucault to avoid what he calls the "blackmail of the Enlightenment," the idea that "one has to be 'for' or 'against' the Enlightenment."[4] The Enlightenment is thus seen—not as an expression of transcendental truths overseeing our destiny but as an integral part of the discursive practices of a specific age. Indeed, explanatory schemes advanced in terms of such truths are the main obstacles in the path toward a more precise understanding of the constraints and conditions overseeing the production of these truths. These themes are precisely the "subjects" that prevent us from understanding discursive practice in the manner already indicated by Ernst Cassirer who saw discourses as an integral part of the "autonomous universe of 'discourse-as-thought.'" Only Cassirer did not go far enough, Foucault thought; consequently, he supposed, "it will no doubt be necessary—and that will be our task—to free ourselves from these limits that are still an unfortunate reminder of the traditional histories of ideas; we will have to learn to recognize thought within its anonymous constraints, to track it down in all the mute things and gestures that give it a positive figure, and to let it unfurl in this dimension of anonymity where each individual, each discourse, forms nothing more than the episode of a reflection."[5] Accordingly, Foucault proposed, "we must treat the instances of discourse that articulate what we think, say, and do, as so many historical events."[6] It is an approach that would permit the individualization of discourses by freeing them from the context of universal themes that posit notions of human essence in religious, political, and scientific discursive practices. Consequently, Foucault proposes that we proceed to develop what he calls a historical ontology of ourselves, an inquiry that will avoid projects that pretend to disclose hidden reasons orchestrating events in this world. As a number of critics have noted, Foucault's approach, in this case, is clearly Nietzschean in its drift. Michael Mahon points out, for example, that "both Nietzsche and Foucault oppose the division of the world into real and apparent. Everything is mediated by the life and consciousness of knowers. All truth is truth for a form of life. All reason is practical reason. Both, therefore, question any allegedly pure and autonomous search for truth, as manifest for Nietzsche in the Stoics and the modern physicists, for Foucault in the Enlightenment."[7]

To counteract this legacy of the Enlightenment, which is the tendency to represent reality, to express the truth of human experience in terms of a reason that derives its validity from the essence that is deemed to constitute our very humanity, Foucault develops various tactics aimed at disclosing the processes of mediation and constraints that operate whenever knowledge is formed and truths are asserted. The first step is to dismantle accepted ways of thought, to "take out of circulation the thoughtless continuities through which discourses to be analyzed are organized in advance . . . to show that they do not happen just like that, that they are always the effect of a construction whose rules have to be determined and whose justifications have to be controlled."[8]

It is in this regard that Kant's question about the Enlightenment is still relevant for us because it provides us with a new model for criticism, which "has to be conceived as an attitude, an ethos, a philosophical life."[9] For Foucault, however, it is a critical attitude that does not seek to disclose transcendental grounds for reason but strives to uncover connections between the discursive and nondiscursive determinants of the established rationality. Indeed, suggests Foucault, it is hardly possible to separate the rationality from the mechanisms it has helped put in place; the question then becomes, "How are we to separate this rationality from the mechanisms, procedures, techniques, and effects of power that determine it, which we no longer accept and which we point to as the form of oppression typical of capitalist societies, and perhaps of socialist societies too?" The disclosure of these connections is also what helps us demystify the ideological pretense of reason and Foucault ends up wondering, "Couldn't it be concluded that the promise of *Aufklärung* (Enlightenment), of attaining freedom through the exercise of reason, has been, on the contrary, overturned, reversing itself into a domination of Reason itself, that it is taking more and more the place of freedom?"[10]

Foucault's underlying premise is that we are kept from seeing the constraints to which we are subjected by a reliance on themes of continuity and conscious agency. He therefore wishes to argue that the traditional representation of human history and agency are part of the same strategy of obfuscation: "The making of historical analysis into a discourse of continuity and the making of human consciousness into the originating subject of all becoming and all practice, these are the two sides of the same system of thought."[11] Once the commonsensical assumptions governing the production of meaning and the representation of reality have been swept aside, space has been cleared for radically different ways of conceptualizing our relation to thought:

> If, as regards history, and precisely as regards the history of knowledge, or of reason, we can show that it does not at all follow the same model as consciousness; if we can show that the time of knowledge or of discourse is not at all organised or disposed in the manner of time as it is lived; that it presents specific discontinuities and transformations; if, finally, we show that there is no need to pass by way of the subject to analyze the history of acquired knowledge, we raise great difficulties, but we are dealing perhaps with an important problem.[12]

Foucault realizes that in carrying out such a design, he is going against a deeply ingrained Western habit of thought and has to confront an ever-present "refusal to recognize that in discourse something is formed, according to clearly definable rules; that this something exists, subsists, changes, disappears, according to equally definable rules; in short, that alongside everything a society can produce (alongside: that is to say, in a determinate relationship with) there is the formation and transformation of 'things said.'"[13] Foucault posits thus a dual system of effective rationalities and wishes to show that the history of knowledge may well follow a pattern and be determined by factors that consciousness ignores. Foucault's tactic is therefore "to relate discourse not to a thought, mind or subject which engendered it, but to a practical field in which it is deployed."[14] What is important then is not what a subject claims or thinks it is saying but what is said unbeknownst to the speaking subject.

To gain such a perspective, it is necessary to reject the theme of a founding subject. For Foucault, it is a necessity that imposes itself in terms of a choice to be made in the context of his genealogical approach: it is necessary to choose between two viewpoints that are fundamentally irreconcilable—the subject's and the discourse's. When Foucault, echoing Beckett, suggests that "in every sentence there reigns the nameless law, the blank indifference:

'What matter who is speaking; someone said: what matter who is speaking,'"[15] it is to call to our attention the way discourse functions independently of the subject. What is revealed, in the absence of a subject that guarantees the meaning of discourse, is precisely the hermeneutical dimension of all signification, the fact that the sign already implies a previous interpretation. The elimination of the subject helps reveal that the formation and transformation of "things said" follow their own rules and partake of a systematicness that is all their own. Consequently, for Foucault, discourse is "that which is actually said, unbeknownst to the speakers: the latter think they are speaking broadly and freely, while, without realizing it, they say things that are narrow, limited by an incongruous grammar."[16]

The realization that our comprehension is preformed produces a radically changed perspective on the production of knowledge and the elaboration of meaning. Also enhanced is a suspicion with regard to the role language plays in the constitution of our beliefs and perceptions; it is, notes Foucault, "the suspicion that language does not say exactly what it says"; that "it overflows, in a sense, its strictly verbal form, and that there are many other things in the world that speak, and that do not belong to language."[17] In addition, this approach makes it possible to elaborate "a history of discursive practices in the specific relationships which link them to other practices."[18] What Foucault wishes to develop and illustrate in this manner is the idea that discourse "must not be taken to be the totality of things said, nor the manner of saying them. It is just as much in what is not said, or what is conveyed by gestures, attitudes, ways of being, patterns of behavior, spacial arrangements." In short, he suggests, "discourse is the totality of the constrained and constraining meanings that pass through social relations."[19]

The representation of these relations or of society, or of history, is only part of the story, however. Foucault also wishes to bring to light the manner in which representation functions in terms of the effects that constitute the silent and, because it is nondiscursive, the often unacknowledged side of a society's history. In considering discourses in terms of a dimension that escapes a conscious apprehension of their meaning, he wishes to highlight a particular discrepancy that accounts for a discourse's impact. Discourse is not so much a plenitude as a lack or a distancing; discourse, he explains, "is constituted by the difference between what one could say correctly at one period (under the rules of grammar and logic) and what is actually said."[20] While speakers labor under the constraints of what passes for the grammatically or politically correct at any given historical period, they are actually producing meanings that are always/already shaped by relations and practices of which they are but dimly aware if at all.

At the same time, the discursive and nondiscursive realms are hardly autonomous: they coexist in ways that defy our current understanding of these processes. By investigating the relationships that link discursive practices to other practices, Foucault ventures into a territory that has remained largely unexplored: "My general theme isn't society but the discourse of true and false, by which I mean the correlative formations of domains and objects and of the verifiable, falsifiable discourse that bear on them; and it's not just their formation that interests me, but the effects in the real to which they are linked."[21] Thus, for example, discourse has an effect on the real because it involves forces that operate through discursive and nondiscursive deployment of strategies of domination and resistance: "For relations of forces, discourse is not only a surface of inscription, but an operator," he points out. Thus, discourse can indeed be seen as "both a place and an instrument of confrontation."[22]

Obviously, according to such a concept of discourse, *what* is said is determined less by a subjective intentionality than by a network of determinants that has its own history and conditions of existence. The relative importance of speaker and what is spoken is therefore inverted. The object of critique is no longer to investigate the motives or rationale of the speaker but to find out how what is spoken is articulated with discursive and nondiscursive practices of the period in question. This concept of articulation is central to the critique of the Enlightenment outlined by Foucault. We know, he tells us, "that the great promise or the great hope of the eighteenth century, or of a part of the eighteenth century, lay in the simultaneous and proportional growth of the technical capacity for acting on things and of the freedom individuals would enjoy with respect to one another." It turned out, however, that "the relations between the growth of capabilities and the growth of autonomy are not as simple as the eighteenth century may have believed."[23] What the Age of Reason could not foresee, was the unavoidable opposition that would arise between technical progress and the freedom of individuals. Consequently, for Foucault, the key for developing an effective critique of the modern age is to know the answer to

"How can the growth of capabilities be disconnected from the intensification of power relations?"[24] The connection between techniques and power has for a long time been occluded by the discourse of progress; Foucault finds, therefore, that a progressive critical strategy would consist of questioning "all the dynamic, biological, evolutionary metaphors that have served to mask the difficult problem of historical change."[25]

As he seeks to disclose the dissimulation of the violence that is implicit in discourse, Foucault recognizes the influence of three masters of suspicion whom he credits with a founding role in this regard. And he supposes that, if we have become aware that signs pretend to be something they are not, it is because "beginning with the nineteenth century, beginning with Freud, Marx, and Nietzsche, it seems to me that the sign becomes hostile; I mean that there is, in the sign, an ambiguous and somewhat suspicious manner of intending, of meaning harm. And this, to the extent that the sign is already an interpretation that doesn't display itself as such. Signs are interpretations that try to justify themselves, and not the reverse."[26] The fact that interpretation is kept hidden also suggests that it is to someone's advantage to cover up the procedure and to deny the fact that signification is dependent on an earlier step. In the wake of the critical work by Nietzsche, Marx, and Freud, the sign loses its innocent autonomy and "interpretation will henceforth always be interpretation by the 'who?'; what is being interpreted, finally, is not what is in the signified, but who posed the interpretation."[27] Nietzsche, for example, showed that words have a history that makes them enter into collusion with specific class interests; thus, "words have always been invented by the upper classes; they do not indicate a signified, they impose an interpretation." As a result, discursive practices are suffused with a violence that is integral to their deployment and "underneath everything that speaks, there never ceases to be the great web of violent interpretations. It is for this reason that there are signs, signs that prescribe to us the interpretation of their interpretation, that prescribe to us to turn them over as signs."[28]

Signs still need to justify themselves, to establish their own legitimacy, their claim to authenticity, in order to hide the fact that "everything is already an interpretation, each sign is in itself, not the thing offered to interpretation, but the interpretation of other signs. There is never, if you will, an *interpretandum* that is not already an *interpretans*."[29] Consequently, the suspicion toward language turns into a critical project whose purpose is to bring the procedures of legitimization to light, to uncover the processes of naturalization and institutionalization whose purpose is to occlude the interpretive moment under the pretense of a rational and objective application of meaning to reality.

What is brought to light, in the investigation of such processes, are the multiple constraints and practices that have evolved according to a logic of their own and that operate both in conjunction with but independently of the highly visible and official discourse of reason. As Roger Chartier points out, Foucault's notable merit is to have demonstrated that "one cannot reduce the practices that make up the social world to the 'rationality' that governs discourses. The logic commanding the operations that construct institutions, dominations, and relations is not the same hermeneutic, logocentric, scriptural logic that produces discourses. That practices, articulated with but homologous to discourses, are irreducible to discourses can be considered the fundamental partitioning principle in all cultural history."[30] From this perspective, "there are no historical objects that preexist the relations that constitute them."[31] The illusion that objects exist somewhere out there, pregnant with meaning, just waiting for someone to decipher them is due to the self-deluding work of consciousness. A self-constituting and self-limiting subjectivity rationalizes such objects retroactively by incorporating them in an overall scheme, thus justifying and validating them after the fact and in terms of the very scheme it creates: "Thus Foucault traces a perspective for historical comprehension that uncouples the significance of the event and the consciousness of individuals."[32] The real, Foucault shows, is as much in discourse as in whatever discourse purports to represent. Moreover, discourse does not necessarily appropriate or assimilate the objects of its representation; the ineffable real is just as likely to coopt discourse itself. This perspective is particularly helpful for gaining a better understanding of the Enlightenment, as Chartier suggests: "Thinking the Enlightenment as a sheaf of practices without discourse (or outside of discourse)—in any event, of practices irreducible to the ideological affirmations intended to justify them—is perhaps the surest way to avoid teleological readings of the French eighteenth century."[33]

Ideology, as Foucault sees it, is a convenient rationalization and idealization, it is like a vast drapery that can be made to fit all circumstances. It is typically used to cover up events according to its special interpretative scheme; it can do this because it posits objects of discourse as things that exist before discourse itself. To avoid being taken in by this subterfuge, Foucault proposes, we must understand that objects are coterminous with the practice that gives rise to them; thus a discursive object "does not preexist itself. . . . It exists within the positive conditions of a complex web of relations."[34] These are the relationships an enunciative function activates at various levels—institutional, economic, and social, it is a "field of exteriority" of multiple relations "established between institutions, economic and social processes, forms of behavior, systems of norms, techniques, types of classification, modes of characterization."[35] And, Foucault adds, these are relations that are not to be found in the object itself; that is why it is important to "interrogate language, not in the direction in which it refers, but in the dimension that gives rise to it," a dimension that incorporates the vast areas of the unknown.[36] As Roger Chartier has suggested, this vast and obscure world of "teeming facts, multiple intentions, interlocking actions thus cannot be ascribed to any system of determinations capable of giving a rational interpretation of them—that is, of pronouncing on their meaning and their causes."[37]

It is this discrepancy between a discursive cover-up of the real and the multiplicity of rationales informing what passes for reality that interests Foucault; like Gadamer, he also appreciates the persistence of tradition, but for him it takes on distinctly political implications, because tradition can turn into domination. The ideology of the Enlightenment, for example, has served as a cover for processes that are yet to be fully understood, and Foucault points out that "the great forms of statehood that developed beginning with the eighteenth century have justified themselves much more in terms of guaranteed freedom than of implanted mechanisms of power, and it is perhaps because these little mechanisms of power had something humble and shameful about them that they were not considered worthy of being analyzed and told."[38] For example, one traditional practice that has insinuated itself as a mechanism of power in modern society, is the pastoral power deployed by Christian religious institutions: "Beginning with the eighteenth century, capitalist and industrial societies as much as the modern forms of State that accompanied and supported them had need of procedures, mechanisms, essentially procedures of individualization that the religious pastorate had put into operation." As a result, under the cover of an officially proclaimed emancipation, "there was an implantation, even a multiplication and diffusion of pastoral techniques within the secular framework of the State apparatus."[39]

The phenomenon of change, as a consequence, presents itself in an entirely different manner—not in terms of imaginary causes attributable to the thoughts and actions of fully conscious and willful subjects, but from the perspective of the substance of change. That is why, explains Foucault, it is important to "define with the greatest care the transformations that have, I do not say: provoked, but *constituted* change."[40] What must be stressed therefore, is what he calls "the wild fact of change," an unpredictability that is ordinarily dissimulated by traditional mental constructs and habits of thought. To get rid of these, it is necessary to "liberate the discursive field from the historical-transcendental structure which nineteenth-century philosophy imposed on it." Since it is no longer the identity of the subject that is revealed in a discourse, the task of the historian is not to relate everything in terms of such familiar forms of thought as "tradition and invention," or "the old and the new," or "the static and the dynamic"; it consists, rather, of telling "the history of ideas as a set of specified and descriptive forms of nonidentity."[41] A paradoxical and difficult task, this goes without saying. It is a task, nevertheless, that has become unavoidable, since it is driven by a conceptualization of discourse that is no longer beholden to the founding principles of modernity.

Foucault's approach, as a number of critics have observed, is fundamentally inseparable from ethics. Thus he often returns to the idea of the philosophical ethos inherent in the critical ontology of ourselves. He defines this ontology as "the historical analysis of the limits that are imposed on us and an experiment with the possibility of going beyond them."[42] It is when it functions to uncover and to discredit procedures of subjectification that this work by ourselves on ourselves becomes a hermeneutics, an analysis of the formations of meaning that summon us to turn into subjects according to the three axes defined by Foucault, namely, "How are we constituted as subjects of our knowledge? How are we constituted as subjects who exercise or submit to power relations? How are we constituted as moral subjects of our actions?"[43] This approach is also genealogical, because "it will not deduce from the form of what we are what it is impossible for us to do or to know; but it will separate out, from the contingency that has made us what we are, the possibility of no longer being, doing, or thinking what we are, do, or think."[44]

It is a critical task that is constantly to be taken up anew, since it is not possible for us to understand or to control the situation of comprehension that is ours: "The theoretical and practical experience that we have of our limits and of the possibility of moving beyond them is always limited and determined; thus we are always in the position of beginning again."[45] The faculty of reason that helps us uncover our limits is also the reason that imposes them; it is an ambiguity that is a characteristic of the functioning of reason and that has remained occluded for a long time by a certain representation of the Enlightenment. Discredited in the name of various positivisms, it reemerges today, and it is under the sign of this ambiguity that the Enlightenment returns, as Foucault noted in the very last essay he had the opportunity to revise before his untimely death:

> Two centuries after it appeared, the Enlightenment returns: both as a way for the West to become aware of its present possibilities and of the freedoms to which it can have access, but also as a way of questioning its own limits and the power it has used. Reason—both as despotism and as light.[46]

6

REASON IN THE
AGE OF ATROCITY

The disintegration of modernity's axiological convictions is indicated most strikingly perhaps by the discredit into which Karl Marx's famous admonition to philosophers has fallen. Philosophers, he claimed, had only interpreted the world; the point really was to change it. The quip evokes a confidence that has since severely eroded. The transformations the world has undergone have generally proven so unsettling and unpredictable that claims to initiate and control change will inevitably meet with skepticism today. In a wider sense, it is the whole project of the Enlightenment with its promise of progress and emancipation that is increasingly brought into question and philosophers, as a result, are more likely to be intent on understanding and interpreting the world than on changing it.

One of the signal developments marking the passage from a modern to a postmodern stage in our civilization has been the critical attention paid to modernity. The reexamination of this era has inevitably tended to dwell on its failings and, in particular, on the relation between an ideology of modernity and the deployment of totalitarian forms of political thought. As we look back on this, the last century of the modern era, we note that the scope of the humanities has become expanded by a new literary genre—due precisely to the unleashing of a violence peculiar to this age: it is the literature authored by the victims of State-sponsored terror. Thus, in his introduction to the memoirs of Nikolai Bukharin's widow, Stephen Cohen, the director of Russian Studies at Princeton, underscores the importance of the vast literary output occasioned by the experience of Soviet slave labor camps: "Gulag literature, much of it written secretly decades ago and only recently freed from censorship, continues to appear. It may be, with its counterpart from the other defining holocaust of modern times, the most characteristic writing of the twentieth century."[1]

A generic concept that would encompass the literatures of the two holocausts can of course be easily extended to include other instances of State-sanctioned repression, torture, and genocide. Indeed, if we take into account the whole literary record of inhumanity for our time, we may begin to suspect, as Carolyn Forché notes in her book *Against Forgetting*, that the twentieth century may well go down in history as the "age of atrocity." What distinguishes primarily this genre from all others is the purpose motivating its authors. The principal function of literary works by the victims of inhumanity and barbarism, is to serve, in the words of Carolyn Forché, "as poetic witness to the dark times in which they lived."[2] In addition, it is the sort of writing that bears witness to the rationales and conditions that made the institution of repression possible, even inevitable. Accounts by inmates of the gulag, for example, typically include reflections on the ethical, philosophical, and political implications of the slave-labor camp experience.

Among the more remarkable narratives of this kind is a two-volume set of reminiscences by Eugenia Semyonovna Ginzburg entitled *Journey into the Whirlwind* and *Within the Whirlwind*, published in English in 1967 and 1981, respectively.[3] A loyal member of the Communist Party and the wife of an important Party official, Ginzberg was arrested in 1937 on an imaginary charge of "terrorism" and spent eighteen years in the infamous prison and slave-labor camp network that became the distinguishing characteristic of Stalin's reign. Her memoirs are an extraordinary account of the ordeal she endured and survived. As she explains in the epilogue, the project of a literary account of her experiences took shape from the very beginning: "Readers often ask me: 'How could you keep such a mass of names, facts, place names, and poems in your memory?' Very simply: because just remembering it all to record it later had been the main object of my life throughout those eighteen years. The collection of material for this book began from the moment when I first crossed the threshold of the NKVD's Inner Prison in Kazan" (II, 418). Having been trained as a teacher and journalist, Ginzburg is quite naturally motivated by a desire to inform her readers and to transmit the knowledge and insights her experience has given her. At the same time, she admits to not comprehending herself what she has gone through and notes that during those eighteen years, the dominant feeling "was that of amazement. Was all this imaginable—was it really happening, could it be intended?" (I, 417). She realizes therefore that time will have to pass before the enormity, the unreality, and absurd irrationality of the whole age she had to traverse will become accessible to reason. As she points out, "When I wrote this record, I thought of it as a letter to my grandson. I supposed that by 1980, when he would be twenty years old, these matters might seem remote enough to be safely divulged" (I, 7).

At the root of the feeling of absurdity was the inability or, in many cases, the refusal to accept a plausible reason behind the extraordinary waves of repression that swept through the Soviet Union in the 1930s and 1940s. What could not be grasped by those who were caught in the events of those times was that they constituted the culmination of an extraordinary experiment at social engineering. In this sense, Soviet society provides a revealing case-study of a systematic development and application of a pretense of civilization. To carry out the project, the whole society had to be subjected to a massive and thorough process of indoctrination. As the Polish dissident Adam Michnik described it: "Attempts to capture control of the human mind are a fundamental feature of the regime under which I live. Such attempts begin in grade school when a spiritual world in which everything is clear, unambiguous, and 'defined to the last detail' is systematically constructed."[4] The unavoidable component in such a project of total thought-control was a system of repression for ensuring the observance of correct thinking. Thus the purpose of the whole Soviet experiment was nothing less than a radical—Orwellian, we might say—transformation of the very process through which truth and reality are ascertained. It was the crowning achievement of Stalinism.

To understand Stalinism, as Slavoj Zizek has shown, it is necessary to take into account a basic distinction concerning the notion of truth in Russian:

> The equivalent of *truth* is *istina*, a word that covers at the same time the abstract notion of truth and the concrete reality to which it applies. *Pravda*, on the other hand, represents a purely Russian concept, that of a superior truth elevated to the status of idea. For the NKVD as

> for the Party, truth expressed by *istina* did not exist: it
> was a thoroughly relative notion, thus easily modifiable.
> Only *pravda* was absolute truth. . . . The concept of
> *pravda* had become the foundation of power . . . and
> everything that did not fit into this framework is *not
> objectively* true.[5]

Objectivity is guaranteed by the Party. Similarly, according to this logic, true freedom is "nothing other than 'a necessity understood,' which is the freedom to recognize and to want 'freely' that which is 'objectively necessary.'"[6]

It is in this sense that Stalinist discourse is, properly speaking, psychotic because it is predicated on a simultaneous acceptance of an official "realism" determined by the application of raw power and denial of reality: "The delirium proper to Stalinist discourse consists in forcing us to deny *istina* in the name of *pravda*, that is, to make us confront an untenable choice: either we deny *reality* in the name of *pravda*, or we are *outside* the Party, in the horrifying *Real*."[7] Far from representing a weakness of Stalinism, it is a contradiction that constitutes its force, Zizek notes: it is what makes fanaticism inevitable. Ironically, it is also at this juncture that it is possible to establish a connection between Stalinism and the Enlightenment:

> Here is the moment—as paradoxical as it might appear—
> when Stalinist discourse becomes heir to the Enlighten-
> ment, they both share the same presupposition of a
> universal and uniform "reason" that even the most
> abject trotskyite refuse is capable of "understanding"—
> and thus of "admitting." Stalinist discourse is a kind of
> "terrorism" of this universal "reason"—all dilemmas are
> transformed in it already in advance under the guise of
> "evidence." Consequently, power intervenes in dis-
> course at the point where we least expected it: in the
> form of an instance of an objective-neutral knowledge,
> outside discourse, not marked by difference . . . in the
> form of an "objective reality" that legitimates power, of
> the "objective meaning" of your actions, etc.[8]

It was a casuistry that victims of Stalinist terror would learn to assimilate gradually, in the experience of interrogations, internment, and exile.

The event that served as pretext for the first purges and set into motion the whole apparatus of terror that was to devour millions was the murder of one man. As Ginzburg notes in her first sentence, the year of her arrest, 1937, "began, to all intents and purposes, at the end of 1934—to be exact, on the first of December" (I, 3). It was the day when Kirov, one of Stalin's close associates and his greatest rival, was assassinated. At the close of her narrative, Ginzburg returns once more to the incomprehensible discrepancy between this event and its consequences by noting that, although she, along with millions of others, had been condemned for acts of terrorism, "after all, despite the millions of terrorists, no one, absolutely *no one* had been killed . . . Only Kirov . . . And all of us in the camps knew the name of his murderer perfectly well" (II, 414). What was—and still is, for many—impossible to comprehend is the simple fact that this murder, as Robert Conquest points out, "was made the central justification for the whole theory of Stalinism and the necessity for endless terror." Within a few years, the project to uncover the plot behind the murder reached truly fantastic proportions and the alleged plotters and their organizations multiplied at a dizzying rate: "The new victims were in one way or another implicated in the Trotskyite-Zinovievite-Rightist bourgeois-nationalist conspiracies (entered into collaboration with the Nazi, the Polish, the Japanese, the British, and other espionage services), whose murder of Kirov had been their most important and characteristic crime. In the end, millions must have been the accomplices, at least to this extent, in the murder."[9]

The fervent dedication with which so many strove to elaborate and shore up a pretense that would justify what amounts to the vastest project of auto-genocide in human history points to a lemminglike unwillingness or inability to accept what was plainly evident. Thus, even at the height of the purges many of the victims stubbornly denied the obvious and numerous inmates of the camps clung to the belief that Stalin was simply not aware of what was going on in the country. As Ginzburg remembers, it was humanly not possible to comprehend and even less to accept the scope and the gratuitous deadly violence of a system whose justifications were purely imaginary in nature. The accusations were all trumped up, thus the crimes had to be invented and the evidence fabricated. That is why the confessions and denunciations extracted from the victims became an essential part of the terror. One former member of the secret police remembers that there were charts of various counterrevolutionary organizations on the walls of NKVD offices and explains: "These organizations were, of course, totally imaginary. But arrested people had to be charged with being agents of something." One of the most common accusations was the charge of spying for a foreign power. However, "for rural, western Siberia, with few factories or nearby foreign powers, this wouldn't do. Instead, it was decided that the major enemy was to be a group 'called the Counterrevolutionary Cadet Monarchist Organization.'"[10] Thus the limits for the scope and intensity of the terror were simply those of the ingenuity and imagination of the party functionaries in charge of the arrests and deportations. As a result, the whole enterprise of repression took on a life of its own, developing along a certain economy of productivity and efficiency that followed its own rules. The NKVD became, in effect, "a regular state department, which had a quota of a certain number of people to arrest."[11]

While the whole State apparatus was increasingly falling under the rule of a murderous and paranoid Imaginary, truth had been driven underground or had taken refuge in the sites of arrest and internment. Thus, paradoxically, it was in the camps where the truth of the situation was most likely to emerge, and a former inmate remembers that "camp was the only place in this country where a person could think freely and talk freely. In camp, people who tried to unravel what was going on had the scales fall from their eyes."[12] For Ginzburg, this truth to be uncovered only in the camps becomes an obsession—it is the ultimate purpose of her writing, as she explains in her epilogue: "So I have written down the truth. Not the *whole truth* (for that I could hardly have hoped to know) but *nothing but the truth*." To accomplish this, she realizes, she had to overcome the ingrained habits of the devoted Party member that she was: "All I could do was to resist subordinating my story to nimble sophisms about what was and what was not expedient, to calculations about what was called for by the needs of the moment" (II, 420–21). In other words, she had to force herself not to rationalize, she had to resist the recourse to the imaginary alibis and ideological sophistry that served to cover up the irrationality and barbarism of the vast inquisitorial apparatus of repression that was engulfing her country. What made it particularly difficult for her and her fellow inmates to accept the unadorned truth of the situation, she realizes, were the very qualities that had made them into fervent revolutionaries in the first place: "We were creatures of our time, of the epoch of magnificent illusions. . . . for all our youthful devotion to the cold formulas of dialectical materialism, we were out-and-out idealists." But, she also notes that, inevitably, "under the blows of the inhuman machine that descended upon us, many of the 'truths' we had been parroting all those years lost their sparkle" (II, 100). She understands that her experience, though brutal and harsh in the extreme, was in effect an educational one: she had to learn that her world of values had been turned upside down—the true had become false, right had turned into wrong, the rational had given way to the absurd. Thus she remembers that in the early stages of her interrogation she still behaved as if the world were governed by reason and logic: "My way of defending myself—by fervent protestation of innocence and loyalty, vainly made to sadists, or officials who were themselves bewildered by the fantastic course of events and terrified for their own skin—was the most absurd of any I could have chosen" (I, 24). She finally had to accept that the system had coopted logic itself when she saw that, ultimately, her fate was sealed by a theoretical argument commonly used in 1937. As one of her interrogators explained to her, "When you get down to it, there is no difference between 'subjective,' and 'objective.'" And Ginzburg, along with millions of others had to adapt to a reality that no longer fit conventional logic—one could be part of a conspiracy against the State without knowing, without having done anything: "Whether you had committed a crime or, out of inadvertence or lack of vigilance, 'added grist' to the criminal's mill, you were equally guilty. Even if you had not the slightest idea of what was going on, it was the same" (I, 32–33).

In a world ruled by such Orwellian precepts, attitudes ranged between two extremes. At one extreme were those who tried to accommodate this world; at the other were the ones who lived with the lucidity brought on by the shattering of illusions. Ginzburg discovers that, just as there is a class of "sadists and bureaucrats" that has emerged with the system, there is also a community of likeminded individuals who share an understanding of life made possible by a certain intellectual and spiritual capacity for filtering the experience of extremity. This common bond comes to her as a revelation when, having served her time in the gulag, she meets former prisoners. "I have never forgotten the sheer joy that my encounter with them brought me," she tells us, adding: "My guests and I were gratified to find that under conditions of identical sufferings and humiliation our thoughts and feelings had developed in the same direction and had brought us more often than not to identical conclusions" (II, 236).

The intellectual lucidity and the spiritual strength that Ginzburg both admires and exemplifies partake, moreover, of a distinctly literary character. She relates this spiritual quality and strength to a cultural legacy whose power she grows to appreciate in the camps where, she says, "no blizzards could extinguish that candle flickering in the wind, the spirituality of the Russian intelligentsia, which my generation accepted as a secret gift from the thinkers and poets of the beginning of the century who had themselves been the targets of our critical shafts" (II, 100). It was this legacy, Ginzburg realizes, that helped her and her soul-mates in the camps understand as well as survive: "It was with the greatest difficulty that our reason, weighed down with ready-made concepts, groped toward the light of reality. Nevertheless, we did manage to carry our 'lighted candles' into solitary confinement, into the huts and punishment cells, and through the blizzard-lashed marches in Kolyma. Those lamps of ours alone were what enabled us to emerge from the pitch-darkness" (II, 100–01). First and foremost, the poetry she knows by heart helps Ginzburg retain a sense of reality. The poems of Blok, Akhmatova, Pasternak, and Mandelstam, as well as the ones she composes herself, help her preserve her humanity. This love of literature is also what creates bonds of love and empathy among fellow-victims and rekindles an appreciation for the value of life in them. Thus, after Ginzburg discovers the joy of a new friendship, she muses: "It was not only our common love of books that brought us together. We instantly sensed in each other an agonized need to think about life, for all its obvious lack of sanity. To hold it up to the light and examine it, to make comparisons and derive general conclusions . . ." (II, 52–53).

At the same time, Ginzburg makes it clear that this way of looking at life both marked and condemned her and those like her and she has numerous occasions to note "the animal hatred of the authorities for the intelligentsia" (II, 228). The hatred is instinctive and also belongs to the logic of the system because it finds its justification in it. Those condemned for political crimes—that is, for the most part, the intellectuals—are, by definition the lowest of the low. As one interrogator explains to her, enemies of the people are not human beings; as a consequence, "we're allowed to do what we like with them" (I, 66). Moreover, prisoners are nothing more than state property and, on the scale of material values, they are ranked below animals. Those who are in charge and who are thoroughly imbued with the logic of the system have grown to accept such a state of affairs as perfectly natural. Ginzburg comes across a rather striking example of one such individual when she is assigned to work for a director of a state farm for convicts who had been trained as a philosopher and had taught dialectical materialism in a university. Ginzburg explains: "He was no sadist. He derived no satisfaction from our sufferings. He was simply oblivious to them, because in the most sincere way imaginable he did not regard us as human." What in the experience of the victims might be termed as "suffering," "agony," and "dying" was for the director a matter of "wastage" and "wastage among the convict work force was to him no more than a routine malfunction of the production line, akin, shall we say, to the wearing out of a silage cutter" (II, 71). What becomes evident from Ginzburg's account, is that the whole system of institutionalized slavery functioned so smoothly because it had successfully replaced the old-fashioned concept of humanity with an abstract and clearly definable theoretical one that fit the tenets of Party dogma and allowed the camp guards and commanders to carry out their functions with perfectly good consciences.

Thus Ginzburg becomes acquainted with a camp commander whose high moral standards made her administration particularly deadly in its effects. The commandant imposes the harshest penalties for the pettiest of crimes because, explains Ginzburg sarcastically, "such ideologically improper considerations as that those guilty of sacrilege against Socialist property were starving never entered her head. For she was *honest*. She never stole, and she never took bribes. How could she, the incarnation of all these virtues, fail to mete out punishment to any brazen hussy who, while working at a fresh vegetable depot, was caught gnawing one of the state's raw potatoes with such of her teeth as scurvy had spared her?" (II, 76). Ginzburg herself falls victim to a similarly strict and narrow-minded application of moral standards when she is accused of gross immorality for having placed a dying man in the half-empty women's wing of the hospital after the men's wing had become overfilled. The verdict sending her back to life-threatening labor in the taiga condemns her for "attempting to create conditions for vice by means of hospitalizing a prisoner of the male sex in a ward for prisoners of the female sex" (II, 130).

Ginzburg's account makes it clear that the system was especially agreeable to a certain type of character—it suited persons with narrow minds and dogmatic natures, those who were easily captivated by abstractions and the pseudologic of the party dogma. But even narrow-mindedness ran the risk of dissipating if neglected and therefore required periodic reinforcement and renewal; thus, while the former philosopher turned camp director had developed a "fixed belief in the solidity and infallibility of the dogmas and quotations he had learned by heart," these apparently tended to weaken over time and, Ginzburg tells us, "there were times when he began to miss the abstractions he had left behind on the mainland. They had become an organic part of his view of life. And so he enjoyed giving the odd lecture on theoretical questions to the free workers of the state farm" (II, 72). When the camp commanders went into retirement and returned to civilian life, this dogmatic outlook helped them live in serene contentment with the sense of proud accomplishment and meritorious service. Ginzburg's narrative sounds a note of bitterness when she remembers, years later, that the commander with the highly developed sense of moral values "is living out her days in 'well-merited' retirement, is the recipient of a special pension, and has access to the Old Bolsheviks' canteen in Riga, where she often comes across those over whose defenseless, tortured heads she held her ax year in, year out—not only held it, but often let it fall" (II, 77).

What Ginzburg's literary rendering of the slave labor experience brings out, is the logic behind the institutionalized violence of the camps. It shows that the inhumanity and deadly reality of the camps was naturalized, made invisible by a narrow-minded adherence to an abstract, official morality and strict observation of a code of conduct. The combined effect of the discursive pretense and the institutionalized disciplinary mechanisms made of the Soviet penal regime a living hell for those caught in its machinery. Behind the superficial veneer of a disciplinary regime imposed according to a strictly codified set of politicomoral principles stands out the brutality of an utterly barbaric system. The violence of the Soviet system, Ginsburg admits, did not have the undisguised brutality of the Nazi camps of extermination; and yet, she finds that the effect of its more subtle and indirect workings proved to be just as deadly. This is the lesson she learns early on in Kolyma, when she is assigned to a special facility designed to house the children born of the occasional amorous liaison that took place even in the appalling circumstances of the camps. What is almost indescribably cruel in its subtle effects, is the process of systematic dehumanization that works according to a simple, logical set of rules. Thus, the children are cared for, but only in regard to their most basic nutritional and excretory needs. Their emotional or intellectual needs are disregarded: the children are not to be held or comforted, no one reads, sings, or even speaks to them. And Ginzburg concludes:

> They are never to be forgotten, those Elgen children. I'm not saying that there is any comparison between them and, say, the Jewish children in Hitler's empire. Not only were the Elgen children spared extermination in gas chambers, they were even given medical attention. They received all they needed by way of food. It is my duty to emphasize this so as not to depart from the truth by one jot or tittle.
>
> And yet when one calls to mind Elgen's gray, featureless landscape, shrouded in the melancholy of nonexistence, the most fantastic, the most satanic invention of all seems to be those huts with signs saying "Infants' Group," "Toddlers' Group," and "Senior Group." (II, 10–11)

The logical outcome of the system was death. Ginsburg had occasion to observe this reality in various settings and numerous circumstances. As she notes wryly, "It was as if some editor kept sending me off deliberately to assemble material on the most varied circles of hell, where I might witness, sharply lighted, the conflict of characters, actions, and thoughts" (II, 78). What allows her to appreciate the operation of the penal system at its deadliest is also what saves her from certain death herself. Through a number of fortunate circumstances and the intercession of several influential acquaintances, Ginzburg becomes a nurse and a doctor's assistant. It is while working in the various camp dispensaries and hospitals that she grows to fully realize the extent to which the whole medical apparatus and the treatments themselves were no more than a pretense mimicking the function and purpose of medicine. And while her new status was keeping her away from such deadly workplaces as the Burkhala gold mine, she found her situation hard to bear:"I was . . . tormented by the cynicism with which the outward respectability and decorum of our establishment served to cloak the horror within. The little gravel paths and flower beds, the new X-ray unit . . . the clean kitchen and the chefs in their white hats . . . There were even scientific conferences of prisoner-doctors. But beneath the veneer of respectability lay each day's discharge of half-dead patients, those fit for return to murderous Burkhala" (II, 142).

What functioned most efficiently in the hospital was the morgue. But even here, after death, the victims underwent a last, dehumanizing indignity. Because the common criminal convicts in charge of the morgue were too lazy to sew up the corpses after autopsies or to dig graves large enough to hold them, and because they stole the sacks in which the bodies were to be buried, they simply chopped the corpses up in pieces to be thrown in the shallow pits they managed to prepare. Once, when Ginzburg stumbles, unexpectedly, on the grizzly scene of one such burial, her first reaction is to remember that a common nickname for the camps was "the mincing machine": "At the sight of this laden Yakut sleigh, the figurative meaning of the word was suddenly replaced by the all-too-solid literal reality. There they were: chunks of human flesh cut up ready for the gigantic mincer. With horror and astonishment I heard the outburst of my own choking laughter, my own loud sobbing. Then I started to vomit uncontrollably" (II, 143).

Although Ginzburg sometimes experiences such momentary breakdowns and occasional bouts with despair, what is perhaps most remarkable about her account is the faith in the overall goodness of humanity to which she steadfastly clings. And while she was acutely aware, from the very beginning, that she, along with millions of others, was caught in the implacable mechanism of a "dreadful system of baiting, inquisition, and torture" (I, 16), she cannot ignore the fact that she was not crushed by it, that whenever it had seemed she was facing certain death, "each time something intervened, something at first sight accidental, but which was really a manifestation of that Supreme Good which, in spite of everything, rules the world. . . ." (I, 411). And indeed, her experience demonstrates time and again that evil has not triumphed, that the system is not perfect and the process of dehumanization and death has its loopholes: its violence is not all-pervasive but is often mitigated by unexpected manifestations of humanity. One episode is particularly telling, in this regard. Because she also eventually offended the camp commander with the strict sense of moral values, she is sent on a forced march of 70 kilometers without food, adequate clothing, or proper footwear, over the snow-covered taiga, to a remote punishment compound for hardened criminals. First, a guard to whom she has provided medical help slips her a parcel of his own food; a second guard gives her boots in exchange for her street shoes because he has a girlfriend who dreams of having "shoes with heels." Then, the officer in charge of an outpost that marks the halfway point of her journey allows her to spend the night there because he intensely dislikes the commander who has imposed the punishment. When Ginzburg resumes her trek, she cannot suppress a surge of optimism:

> I strode out far more boldly now, thinking as I went along what a godsend for us all the Russian character was. By then we already knew of the Nazi bestialities. I shuddered to think how fearful the combination of cruel decrees and total, unquestioned efficiency must be. It was not quite like that with us! With us there nearly always remained some loophole for ordinary human feelings. Nearly always the decree—however devilish it may have been—was mitigated by the innate good nature of the executors, by their slackness, or simply by trust in the famous Russian "maybe." (II, 98)

In addition to being grateful for the slackness of the Russian character, Ginzburg also values, as we have already seen, the rich spiritual legacy of Russian culture. Along with the poems she herself composes, this literature that she recites to herself as well as to her fellow inmates of the prisons and the camps is what helps her maintain a link with humanity and with sanity. Perhaps the most difficult burden to bear during her years of internment and exile is her separation from her two sons, who are four and ten years old at the time of her arrest. This burden becomes nearly unbearable when she learns of the death of her older son, Alyosha. The restrained tone of her narrative, the sparseness of the prose, make it evident that she finds it very painful to speak about this personal tragedy more than twenty years later. Ginzburg does, however, experience the joy of being reunited with her other son, Vasya. Moreover, when she first sees him after a separation of some twelve years, she makes a thrilling discovery: "I found myself catching my breath with joyful astonishment when that first night he started to recite from memory the very poems that had been my constant companions during my fight for survival in the camps. Like me, he too found in poetry a bulwark against the inhumanity of the real world. Poetry was for him a form of resistance. That night of our first talk together we had Blok and Pasternak and Akhmatova with us" (II, 266–67).

Ginzburg discovers something else that is enormously gratifying to her: her son belongs to those who have understood the truth.

This is revealed to her when they are reunited in the apartment of a member of the NKVD where a party is in full swing. The revelers momentarily interrupt their merrymaking to savor the sentimental drama of this unusual reunion. Ginzburg is on the verge of breaking down, when her son quickly whispers in her ear: "Don't cry in front of them. . . ." She quickly regains her composure:

> I looked at him in the way that those who are really close, who know everything about one another, who are members of the same family, look at one another. He understood my look. It was the most crucial moment in my life: the joining up of the broken links in our chain of time; the recapturing of our organic closeness severed by twelve years of separation, of living among strangers. My son! And he knew, even though I hadn't said a word to him, who *we* were and who *they* were. (II, 265)

It is the difference between those who have prospered from the system and those who have seen through the lies that sustain it. The false sentimentality of the revelers is akin to the superficial and official morality promoted in the camps. These are people incapable of seeing the barbaric reality behind the cover of the official system of values. What Vasya has understood, what Ginzburg's narrative itself reveals, is the gap between the pretense and the ineffable reality: it is the truth that she so fervently wishes to transcribe. It is a literary truth that derives from the symbolic power of language and is most effectively transmitted by forms of literary expression. That is why young Vasya, who had inherited this capacity and intelligence from his mother and was to become a writer himself, knew the truth instinctively.[13]

This truth that Ginzburg's narrative divulges can be situated then at several levels: it concerns a personal experience as well as the pathogenic development of a whole society; it relates to a particular moment in history but it also constitutes a commentary on the human condition. The truth is made possible by suffering, it becomes accessible through the trauma undergone by the author's psyche. But the lucidity is due less to the physical suffering and deprivations than to the upheaval undergone by her system of values, her sense of right and wrong, of truth and falsehood. As she points out at the very beginning of her memoirs, "The successive wounds inflicted on me by the dreadful system of baiting, inquisition, and torture hurt me less than those I suffered when I first came up against it" (I, 16). As a result, her narrative is driven by an obsession to set things aright. To accomplish this aim, she needs to effectuate a reversal: to tell the story of a time when the world had been turned upside down, when absurdity reigned, and a senseless terror had replaced basic notions of humanity with a kind of elemental barbarism, to display the naked brutality of a system that had institutionalized a technology of violence and death, her narrative has to first reject the system's ideological cover. It is the first step in her quest to make sense of a world gone mad. The second stage in this quest consists of finding and reestablishing a redemptive theme for human existence. Ginzburg has, as we have seen, a profound need to believe in some "Supreme Good" ruling the world, one whose manifestations she detects in the occasional humaneness of her guards, in the moral and spiritual qualities of fellow inmates. It is such a fundamental goodness added to an irrepressible optimism that attract Ginzburg to Anton, the German doctor she meets in the camps and whom she eventually marries. She finds it reassuring to hear Anton counter all her cynical arguments about society's descent into an unredeemable barbarism. While not a believer herself, she values the comfort she finds in Anton's unshakable Pascalian faith, which he expresses matter-of-factly after one particularly trying experience: "It's been a terrible day, my dearest. But don't despair. True, man has a beast in him, but the beast cannot triumph over man in the end" (II, 125). Ginzburg's attempt to restore to the world she evokes in her writing a mythical dimension of human goodness can also be seen as an attempt to give new life to something in herself—to rediscover the convictions that once guided her involvement in the politics of her country and to reactivate the faith that supported her youthful idealism. It is of course an idealism that is no longer naive. Her work, in this sense, belongs to the vast corpus of literary and critical writing that speaks of a profound disenchantment with the direction our civilization seems to have taken over the last century and with modernity's propensity to violence in particular. What distinguishes the modern age from previous ones, according to a number of thinkers, is the implication of violence in political thought and action. Hannah Arendt comments on this connection in her essay, *The Human Condition* noting the troubling regularity with which ideals turn deadly:

> This has been particularly striking in the series of revolutions, characteristic of the modern age, all of which—

with the exception of the American Revolution—show the same combination of the old Roman enthusiasm for the foundation of a new body politic with the glorification of violence as the only means for "making" it. Marx's dictum that "violence is the midwife of every old society pregnant with a new one," that is, of all change in history and politics, only sums up the conviction of the whole modern age and draws the consequences of its innermost belief that history is "made" by men as nature is "made" by God.[14]

The collusion of violence and politics has been greatly facilitated by another noteworthy development marking the modern era—the powerfully motivating role achieved by ideology. What many have learned, in the light of painful and bitter experience, is that "ideology is paved with good intentions."[15] For Hannah Arendt, ideology is no more than "the logic of an idea"; it is the pretense of explaining history as a "unique and coherent process."[16] The attempt to realize the pretense, to impose the ideological abstraction as an indisputable truth on a society necessarily brings violence in its wake and often makes ideals turn deadly. "The worst violence," explains the French philosopher Alain Finkielkraut, "is not born of the antagonism that exists among men, but from the certitude to deliver them from this antagonism for ever. . . . It is because it wanted to put end to this reign that Ideology plunged humanity in an unprecedented state of distress."[17] Paradoxically, what makes ideology particularly deadly is its appeal to the highest aspirations of humans, to their sense of morality; thus ideology's "absolute immorality is not due to its cynicism or Machiavellianism, but to the exclusively moral nature of its categories."[18]

It is partly this paradox that has led to a reexamination of the ideological underpinnings of modernity. One of Ginzburg's noteworthy accomplishment is to have demonstrated how readily and easily morality turns deadly when a society becomes divided into the two factions of its defenders and its enemies. At the same time, her work demystifies and demythifies the whole Stalinist enterprise by underscoring the mindlessness of an instrumental rationality whose effectiveness feeds on its own absurdity. The great secret behind the need to institute endless terror is precisely that there is none; there is no conspiracy, there are no crimes to punish. There is only the perceived need to inspire terror for reasons of political expediency, according to a rationale already provided by Nikolai Krylenko, Lenin's Commissar of Justice: "We must execute not only the guilty," he recommended; "execution of the innocent will impress the masses even more."[19] A violence thus unleashed can no longer be restrained because a praxis that becomes its own end is utterly destructive in its absurdity. The viciousness of this circle of self-destructiveness is due inevitably to an unreflected reliance on action for action's sake: "Technology and related forms of human praxis, when turned wholly against nature and humanity itself, function as surrogates of the force they were meant to overcome . . . instrumentality, finally escaping any properly human end, triumphs in potentially nihilistic destruction."[20] What is negated in such a process is the one ethical principle essential for ensuring the survival of human society: the respect for human life. Such a respect is absolutely essential for linking reason to action, Genevieve Even-Granboulan argues:

> *Pragmatism and political realism have no force to oppose to the periodical flare ups of violence;* only a belief in the value of human being can oppose it; that is why it takes a certain kind of political courage to oppose any attempts against this ideal; because, as soon as it is attacked, a breach opens up, letting spew forth this violence that is contained only momentarily and that wants nothing better than to run wild.[21]

Ginzburg wrote her memoirs, as we saw earlier, in the hope that by 1980, Soviet society would have progressed sufficiently to begin to deal with the monumental absurdity of her times. She did not live to see the 1980s, but she would have been disappointed to see that the system of which she was a victim had grown very deep roots indeed. Although the gulag had largely been eliminated by then, the conjunction of rhetoric and denial was as strong as ever. In other words, the mechanism whereby an unchecked deployment of persecutions could be unleashed was still in place. A good illustration of the tenacity of this pattern of denial and self-delusion is to be found in the papers that constitute the proceedings of the twelfth World Congress of Philosophy, held in 1988 in Brighton, England, and organized by the Institute of Philosophy of the USSR Academy of Sciences.[22]

The official theme of the Congress was "The Philosophical Understanding of Human Beings." The editors of the Proceedings point out, accordingly, that all of the papers revolve around the issue of humanism and that all of the contributors agree on one fundamental principle, which is the notion of "man as the goal of social development." As one academician specifies, it is today's most important global issue: "For man is the condition, the goal and the result of social progress" (130). This theme reappears in sometimes sternly scientific, sometimes sentimentally effusive renditions. Thus, one philosopher gushes about striving to create a culture for "man" that will comprise

> not only the wealth of knowledge accumulated by man, an evidence of the development of his reason, but also the development of a whole range of human feelings, and above all a love of mankind, the very capacity for love, for a moral, aesthetic and spiritual life which is objectified not just in museums, in things or any semiotic systems, but in man himself, in the beauty of the human personality, its intellectual riches, in interpersonal relations, in people's way of life and its moral foundations, in man's relations with the whole universe—nature and society. (121)

What will determine the legitimacy of these relations above all is a sound, rational, scientific approach. As the editors also point out, the goal is first and foremost "to analyse facts soberly, to be guided by objective logic." Thus we also find in the opening remarks of Ivan Frolov, the President of the Philosophical Society of the USSR, what amounts to a restatement of the ethos of the Enlightenment: "As the progress of science and the study of philosophical foundations have shown," declares Frolov, "the elaboration of major scientific problems, connected with the cognition of the laws of nature, society and the human mind largely facilitates the solution of urgent problems" (11). Of course, such a rather artless declaration of an unbounded faith in progress and reason makes our worthy president sound more like Pangloss than Voltaire.

Equally striking in their naïveté are the assertions of theoretical infallibility we encounter. "It should be emphasised in this context," intones one participant, "that the national interests of the Soviet people are identical with the common interests of mankind because of the class nature of the Soviet socialist society and the fact that the working class constitutes the leading force in its advancement" (159). Since the epistemological and axiological foundations for the inquiry are secure, it stands to reason that Soviet theoretical thought, according to one philosopher, seeks nothing less than "to provide a comprehensive and objective picture of the complex world of today" (21). The guarantor of objectivity is—of course—the truth of Marxism-Leninism and the search for expanding our knowledge of the world can therefore proceed on the path indicated by these illustrious antecedents: "The twentieth century has exacerbated beyond all measure that conflict between barbarism and civilization and between violence and culture. Lenin's idea on the need for and a possibility of creating associations of people and nations 'by granting advantages, spreading culture, and not by force' is extremely relevant today when we look for ways of development of social thought" (178).

At the same time, the philosophers do recognize that reality is a complicated thing and that discrepancies do exist between the development of individual consciousness and the evolution of social processes. Since "changes in social conditions and the development of man himself are relatively independent processes," as someone observes, there can occur a lag between the two. Consequently, the goal of all good social scientists is clear—it is to coordinate the two: "A harmonious and optimal correlation . . . between the processes of change of objective possibilities and the development of man . . . requires the timely resolution by the most adequate means of the contradictions that arise in this sphere" (124). The coordination between the two turns out to be a one-way process, however, for the simple reason that "processes of change of possibilities" are "objective." The humans who are subject to these processes therefore have to be considered malleable; thus, to facilitate socioeconomic development, it is necessary "to shape man's interests and ideals." But to do it effectively, "It is essential to make a deep study of the objective logic of these processes, to skillfully form the masses' understanding of this development and to take due account of the correlation between ordinary and theoretical consciousness" (27–28). Which is to say that the purpose of the exercise is to make the so-called ordinary consciousness fit the theoretical consciousness.

How is this development to be achieved? Well, the academicians tell us, by emphasizing individuality, by imbuing each subject with a belief in his or her autonomy and mastery. The key to the process is something called "the human factor": "in enhancing the human factor it is of crucial importance to inculcate in every worker the feeling of master everywhere and in all cases, a master who does not wait for the nod of superiors, and approaches life and production with a thrifty eye" (25). What we have here then is Philosophy as the art of managing efficiency and cost-effectiveness in the work place. Moreover, the alleged mastery to be achieved by the individual is clearly beneficial to the system and is meant to ensure its preservation: "The making of man as the purpose of social development, and as an end in itself, presupposes not only the shaping of the human essence in each person through his mastery of the experience of previous generations, but also the creation of new forms of existence. The mastery by individuals of existing forms of culture is only a prerequisite of their development" (122). We may at first find somewhat puzzling this idea of "shaping a human essence" by means of achieving "mastery of the experience of previous generations." The mystery dissipates, however, when we take into account a guiding principle that the editors present as axiomatic for examining and explaining our world: "Today's large-scale, complex issues of social development both in our country and in the world at large require the creative development of the social and philosophical theory on the basis of a thorough study of the great heritage of Marx, Engels and Lenin" (7), they assure us. The mastery in question thus turns out to be another name for indoctrination.

The elaboration of the theoretical apparatus, however, does indeed show considerable creativity, especially in the area of history. One academician, for example, develops a sweeping survey of one hundred years of global transformation by enumerating the major events that have taken place and that can be anticipated in the period 1917–2020. The era is divided into four stages: The first stage (1917–1945) is marked by "the emergence of socialism . . . the beginning of the general crisis of capitalism . . . the destruction of the world colonial system . . . the smashing of fascism," and so on. The second stage (1945–1975) sees "the emergence and extension of the world socialist system" as well as "the elimination of the world colonial system and the attainment of national independence by almost all peoples on Earth" (53). Not a word about the vastest, and frequently the most repressive and deadliest colonial system of all—the Soviet Union. The third "and current stage (1976–2000) is marked by structural changes in most countries' economies" as well as by "a new twist in the development of military and political relations between the socialist and capitalist countries" (53).

The fourth period remains fairly nebulous, promising "further profound and radical socio-political changes in many countries" that would include the development of such new "structures of values" as "labour morals, ideological and ecological values" (54).

Ironically, the description of the third stage turns out to be fairly prophetic: thus, the period 1976–2000 also witnesses "the transition of the more developed socialist countries to intensive and accelerating economic and social development" (53). The speaker does not realize of course the full implications of "the new twist," namely, that the transition would also mean the end of the Soviet Union only three years later. Similar ironies are to be found in other papers whose intention is to detail the superiority of Soviet philosophy but which, in retrospect, point out its self-deluding logic: "Contrary to what the Utopians thought, communism is not an ideal that rests within its own limits of perfection. It is rather a historical movement the prospects of which are determined by its inner logic" (118). We can see today that it is precisely this inner logic of the system that doomed it. It manifests itself throughout the papers of the conference that took place a short three years before the whole system imploded. What these papers manifest then is the almost desperate attempt to cover up an ever-widening discrepancy between the official picture and everyday reality. The attempts at developing a theory, a cognitive apparatus that would somehow patch over this gap are so transparently self-referential and self-serving, the rhetoric so patently shallow that what emerges constantly is the deeply flawed logic, the lack of intellectual acumen, the wooden and archaic conceptual apparatus holding up the whole shaky edifice. Again, the flawed thinking is often pointed out unwittingly by the participants; thus one academician proudly explains that "Cognition is regarded by Marxism as a concrete and constantly developing component of social practice" (65). That was precisely its problem. It was a system of cognition that had to be imposed by force because the social practice on which it founded its legitimacy had long since lost its credibility; the first to realize this were the inhabitants of the gulag, but it was not long before the suspicion that the system was bankrupt became a pervasive trait of the collective consciousness.

What these papers make evident, first, is the decay of a civilization, if we measure civilization in terms of the force, creativity, and depth of its intellectual, and artistic productions. The poverty of ideas manifest in the work of these philosophers is so stunning that the reader cannot help but consider the abysmal depths to which Russian culture had fallen. One is led to suspect indeed that a cultural catastrophe of this magnitude can only be the sign of an impending collapse of the society itself. Second, the conference is yet another indication of the vacuity that disables the rhetoric of the Enlightenment today. Arguments proposing respect for reason and for humanity, professing reverence for universal spiritual and aesthetic values have been abused for so long that they have inevitably lost their powers of conviction. Which means, essentially, that the relation between universal pretexts and particular effects has to be rethought. It is clear that universals can no longer stand on their own. For the eighteenth century, reason was the answer. For us, it has become a fundamental problem. Reason turns out to be a cover for strategies that can work in contradictory ways: it can serve to reveal and thus dispel the systems that hold us in their power as well as impose them; it can discredit violence imposed in its name as well as legitimate it.

7

Ethnic Identity in a Post-Stalinist Age

If the Soviet experiment can be considered as an extreme case of a misappropriation and misuse of Enlightenment ideology, it could also be seen as an example of the power and effectiveness of indoctrination in the maintenance of a pretense. In Lithuania, one of the most popular plays to be performed in Vilnius the year the country gained its independence was a satirical revue that consisted entirely of official Soviet propaganda documents and transcripts of radio broadcasts disseminated in Lithuania over the previous fifty years. Ceslovas Stanys, the creator and director of the play, was fascinated by the reaction of the audience, noting that "audiences are shocked when they hear these texts. They are shocked that people actually wrote and read such idiotic words, and sang these stupid songs to the health of Stalin. Before the performance I always warn the audience that even though they lived through these times, they will be persecuted by one thought as they listen. 'It cannot be.' But it happened, and we became anesthetized to it, because fifty years of Soviet rule in Lithuania drove us out of our minds. Our socialist society was a huge loony bin that turned us into psychic invalids."[1]

The immense popularity of the play could therefore be attributed to its cathartic, curative powers. The reliving of the insanity that marked the era of Soviet occupation has consequently become an important step in the process of regaining a sense of balance and of reconstructing a sense of identity that former victims of the Soviet system evidently need to undergo. It is a process that is particularly evident in countries that have regained their independence

111

in the wake of the Soviet Union's collapse. These are countries that had been slated to disappear as ethnic or national entities. As a consequence, deportation to the gulag and to Siberia had an important practical purpose in this regard. It was undertaken to eliminate that segment of the population most likely to resist the planned genocide and, simultaneously, to make room for the waves of Russian colonizers sent to ensure that the territories along the Baltic would forever remain Russian.[2] In this respect at least, the Soviet experiment had less to do with the creation of a new society than with the accomplishment of a design already pursued by the tsars—which was to open up a window to the West along the shores of the Baltic.

The need to relive the occupation and everything relating to it, painful as it may be, is thus an opportunity to find new ways of coping with reality following the disintegration of the existing political rationales and philosophical pretenses. The literature documenting the experience of the gulag or of deportation has therefore become an important factor in the search for self-renewal. In Latvia, it became a nationwide project shortly before independence was won. On March 25, 1989, a special issue of *Literatura un Maksla* (Literature and Art) commemorated the mass deportations of June 14, 1941 and March 25, 1949, and outlined a systematic project of gathering and publishing materials and personal testimony documenting the experiences of the victims of Stalinism. The newspaper proposed specifically the collection and publication of all available accounts. This task was conceived in terms of three kinds of compendia: one was to include concrete data and would principally draw up lists of victims; another one would reproduce the eyewitness accounts of the victims, as well as photographic and other material evidence; a third kind would be of a purely literary nature and would collect the works of prose and poetry that were generated during the years of internment and forced exile.

In one regard, the proposal put forth by *Literatura un maksla* was moot since it was outlining a project that was well under way already. Indeed, the newspaper itself had by then become one of the most important vehicles for this kind of literature. A similar undertaking was also being considered by other organizations—by societies and clubs founded by the victims of Stalinist repression, by the Latvian Writers' Union, and by committees formed to investigate the crimes of Stalin and his henchmen. What *Literatura un maksla* was doing, in effect, was publicizing an existing project and giving it added impetus by providing it with a clear purpose and legitimate rationale.

The special issue of *Literatura un maksla* also makes the point that the need to document these crimes was especially pressing because time was running out: both victims and their tormentors were growing old and dying out. It was therefore important to gather the testimony of survivors who were still there to remember and it was urgent to begin identifying those officers of the slave labor camps who, after a meritorious and murderous career, had settled in Latvia, to enjoy retirement in the comfort of the most luxurious apartments in Riga and private villas along the Baltic shore. Thus one former inmate of the gulag observes that he finds it particularly galling to hear certain Russians on the streets of Riga using the particular insult aimed at Latvians that was characteristic of the language of labor camp guards.

The most notable result of this project to document the crimes of Stalinism, to date, has been the publication of the four-volume collection entitled *Via dolorosa: Stalinisma upuru liecibas* (The Testimony of Victims of Stalinism, Riga, 1990–1995) edited by Anda Líce. The volumes have assembled some two-thousand pages of materials that include poems, memoirs, personal reflections and recollections, letters, and transcripts of tape-recorded narratives. Some of the authors present their texts in a first draft form and have since published fuller accounts in separate books. These books continue to be written today and the activity is remarkable for its intensity as well as for its orientation. Reviewing the literary output of the previous year in Latvia, Anita Rozkalne notes that "we are submerged in history—our own and the world's. It seems as if we have never been submerged to this extent. Our literature has been looking to the past—for several years now, and our appetite in this regard is still not sated."[3] As Rozkalne points out, the obsession with the past is motivated by two distinct yet closely related concerns: by documenting the empirical experience of a people, historians and other authors strive to situate the evidence of individual as well as communal experiences within the context of a historical pattern—or, in some cases, a destiny. It is in this regard that the literature of deportation, also known as Literature of the Repressed, becomes particularly revealing.

Clearly, it is a literature whose significance overflows merely literary or aesthetic concerns. For some, this peculiar role and function of the literature of the gulag runs the risk of emphasizing the tragedy of individual suffering at the expense of the literary worth of a work. Thus, one critic observes that:

the poet's fate has overtaken the poetry itself . . . Poets
who died—or survived for that matter—under Stalin are
in even greater danger of having the complexity of both
their lives and their work eclipsed by their history and
their age's. The poet's martyrdom or survival may so
dominate perceptions of the life and writing that it
becomes nearly impossible to retrieve the intricacies of
the life as lived, the text as written, from beneath the all-
engulfing shadow of the poet's troubled fate.[4]

But it is also possible to view the literary and the existential as two
mutually supportive and reinforcing aspects of this latest genre. The
editor of *Literatura un Maksla*, Maris Caklais, remembers that,
already two years earlier, after a number of important publications
dealing with the gulag, he was being asked, "Well, shouldn't that
suffice? Don't we have enough of these tales of the calvary?" To
which he answers, "No. And not for a long time to come. We must
learn to appreciate this literature—both as the testimony for an era
and as literature. The works of such authors as Olafs Gutmanis,
Aleksandrs Pelecis, Modris Zihmanis, and Knuts Skujenieks fully
justify this. While these authors represent varying degrees of suffering and literary talent, they deal with an episode that is not to be cir-
cumvented."[5] Indeed, the aesthetic quality of this literature is very
much a function of the trauma it represents and is therefore inseparable from the other qualities that make of the Poetry of Witness the
genre peculiar to our age. It is a literature, as we have seen, that
functions to modify our understanding of literature in general.
Specifically, a literary record of an experience of extremity forces us
to rethink the relations between poetry and politics, between the
"personal" and the "political." Forché thus proposes that "we need
a third term, one that can describe the space between the state and
the supposedly safe havens of the personal." And she proposes that
we call this space "the social," a space to be seen as "a place of resistance and struggle, where books are published, poems read, and
protest disseminated. It is the sphere in which claims against the
political order are made in the name of justice."[6]

It is the very space, I would like to argue, in which identity is
formed and reinforced: an identity transcending the strictly personal affiliations and identifications yet more intimate than any
sense of a purely national allegiance. It is an identity that feeds on
the empirical evidence of a past and present experience of a com-

mon fate. For a Latvian poet, this space would define his or her "Latvianness." It is thus through an ironic reversal that justice is done. It is a poetic justice, both literally and figuratively: it was the attempt to erase, eradicate, obliterate this Latvianness that produced the martyrs of Stalinism; today, the literary accounts of the martyrdom serve to validate anew a people's national and cultural identity. All of these texts thus constitute what could be considered a particular genre or subgenre, a mode of literary expression that has its own reason of being, its own special political and cultural significance.

The importance of this literature can be appreciated in several regards. It is, first, a corpus of historical documents that stands as a vivid indictment of an era, a regime, and of all those who were the willing participants in genocide. The memory of deportations is deeply and painfully etched in the collective memory of Latvians. It is estimated that in all, close to 200,000 persons—that is, about ten percent of the adult population—were deported in the 1940s and 1950s.[7] The deportations that took place on June 14, 1941, have been thoroughly documented; there is, for example, the book entitled *These Names Accuse*, which lists the names of some 35,000 victims.[8] We know much less, however, about the victims of the 1949 and other later deportations and, to date, there have appeared relatively few first-person accounts of the experience of deportation.[9] Since the late 1980s, the activity to publish such accounts has intensified and, as a result, we are now able to gauge more fully the scale and range of horrors perpetrated in the name of a brighter future for humankind.

This literature thus bears testimony to crimes committed against humanity. *Via dolorosa* is a most powerful document in this sense. Because it is a collective undertaking, it succeeds in evoking most tellingly the scope and barbarism of the Stalinist enterprise. To put it very simply, deportation was a highly efficient way of torturing people to death. The process was agonizingly painful and slow, yet required little active effort on the part of those responsible. There were of course the few sadists who entertained themselves in various ways by inflicting additional and exceptional doses of agony on some particularly unfortunate individual; in general, however, the conditions in which people had to live and work were sufficient to guarantee prolonged suffering.

The whole process of deportation was designed to be both mentally and physically traumatic in the extreme. From the moment of arrestation, the mental anguish and terror never eased: there was the banging on the door in the middle of the night; at the railroad station fathers and husbands were separated from the rest of the family; everyone was then herded into cattle cars and the long harsh journey toward an unknown fate began. Many Latvians had to undergo this traumatic experience twice; those who were deported in 1941 were allowed to return after the war, only to be deported again in 1949.

The train ride was but a prelude to the hellish reality of Siberia. Whether deportees wound up in the camps or the Siberian villages, existence was generally characterized by conditions that were close to unendurable. There was the constant lack of food, of adequate clothing, there was the unbearable cold and the attendant cases of frostbite that often turned gangrenous; there was the unending infestation by lice and other kinds of vermin, and there were the often deadly illnesses and infections—all conditions that were only aggravated by an inhuman workload. Death, as a result, was the normal and often merciful outcome; although the likelihood of death varied from place to place and was also determined by the age and gender of the deportee. The conditions of deportation were deadliest for men; very few survived, especially the deportation of 1941. For example, in the case of the camp of Vjatlaga, one of the rare instances where such deaths were documented, out of 4,000 Latvian men sent there, about 300 came out alive. To survive, one had to be the beneficiary of unusual luck, or of a special job such as an assignment in bookkeeping or in the camp infirmary, or of some other extraordinary circumstances. For example, if one played on a soccer team organized for the amusement of the guards, one received an extra bowl of soup. A grave digger enjoyed the privilege of licking out the soup bowls of the deceased.

The chances for survival were also slim for the very young. Women, who were sent with their children to various remote outposts of northern Siberia had the best prospects. One of the reasons for this was very simple: these were mothers whose uppermost concern was the survival and well-being of their children; this devotion and willingness to sacrifice their own well-being, even life, provided them with an endurance and strength that often verged on the superhuman. After retelling the horrifying tale of her experiences, one woman puts it very simply: "But we withstood it all—barefoot, without underwear, all the infections, the malaria, the lice, the hunger, the humiliations, because we were thinking of our children. It was a struggle for life, for survival" (414). In addition, the will to sacrifice not only applied in a narrow sense, to members of one's own family, but manifested itself more generally as a sentiment of solidarity and an unselfish concern for others, especially for the young ones: one woman remembers with gratitude the older Latvian women in her camp who willingly and regularly gave up a part of their starvation rations to supplement those of the younger women.

The literature of deportation is also valuable in a way that all literature is: it tells us something about humanity in general. With its dramatic and revealing tales of survival in the face of overwhelming odds and appalling suffering, it discloses as yet unappreciated or unfamiliar facets of human character and potential. Ojars Ozolins, a survivor of the copper and iron ore mines of Dzezkazgana and a contributor to a collection of poems by a literary group of inmates, finds that the poetry in question gives us a valuable insight into "what a human being experiences when he sees himself and his people on the road to annihilation, it reveals the experience of someone who has been condemned to endless years of slave labor but who remains inflexible in his adherence to the eternally ancient spiritual values of his country and his people."[10]

This literature therefore tells us also something about a people, that is, about Latvians. In the first place, it reveals a certain character, a cultural conditioning that was often instrumental in ensuring survival. One is tempted to suppose that one result of seven hundred years of occupation by an assortment of foreign powers has been to develop, through a process of natural selection, both a genetic makeup and a pattern of behavior comprising those characteristics that are necessary for survival in highly unfavorable, even life-threatening circumstances. Singing was one such strategy: "We sang," explains Irene Dumpe, "in order to forget hunger, in order not to cry—songs were our protectors, our saviors, they were dear to us, holy" (343). Although exceedingly rare, humor does occasionally lighten the narrative; a sculptor who is in charge of emptying latrines, decides one day to do a sculpture, with the material at hand—which quickly solidifies in the subzero temperature— a statue of Stalin himself. The guards are thoroughly confused because they cannot decide whether to consider the action as an homage or as blasphemy.

Another important part of this strategy of survival was the process of writing, of recording everyday experiences, of meditating on them and transposing them in poetic form. Poetry was often the preferred medium because poems could be memorized and did not need to be written down. In the camps, only letter writing was allowed, and even then it was restricted—to one or two letters a year, in some cases. Any other kind of writing discovered in the course of the frequent searches was seized and the punishment reserved for the offender could further debilitate an already weakened constitution thus making the chances of survival even more precarious.

At the same time, it is obvious that the fear of discovery was not an effective deterrent because for many, any kind of intellectual or creative activity was as dear as life itself. It was an activity that provided a tenuous but essential link to rationality and humanity; it was an occasion for reflecting on a world gone mad, on a civilization regressing to a stage of utter barbarity. It was also a means of diversion, a way of disciplining one's mind, of turning thoughts away from an existence that threatened at every moment to become utterly unbearable. Moreover, the creative act could also be made to acquire a quasi-magical, incantatory force and thus provide the individual with the capacity to transcend—if only in his or her imagination—the agony of the moment. A poem could become a prayer, or a mantra, a magical ritual that had the power to cast spells, to exorcise evil, and to curse evildoers.

Two themes are particularly common, because they are clearly deemed to possess the evocative force necessary to offset evil and to give the strength to endure. One such theme is the love of nature. Even here, in the frozen and deadly expanses of the polar circle, nature is beautiful and offers comfort; thus army lieutenant Arvids Lasmanis remembers that, "in spite of the suffering, my heart could not help but rejoice at the beautiful skies over the valley of death of Norilska . . . the endless expanse of crystal clear blue skies provided the soul with something akin to a respite, a comfort, a consolation" (96).

Another, even more frequent source of comfort and of strength is the thought of Latvia and the overwhelming, indestructible hope of returning home one day—"The desire for our homeland, for Latvia, was like the air we breathed. It was the main thing on our minds: survive and return," explains Anda Burtniece (207). Even when the return became unlikely in body, it remained a certainty in spirit.

Certain aspects of what could be called a national character— that is, manifestations of a certain kind of cultural conditioning—

are also made manifest in the style in which these accounts are given. The way things are said, what is said, and what remains unsaid can be recognized as aspects of a characteristically Latvian cultural ethos. The dominating literary figure is understatement. There is very little rhetoric, emotional pathos, or invective. Of course, the events themselves are so dramatic that a minimalist rendering of experiences is perhaps the most effective and powerful means of narration. The experiences are also, literally unspeakable, beyond the capacity of human language to express. Thus the simplest, barest prose is deemed adequate. Here, for example, is the account given by Anda Burtniece, who was ten years old when she saw her little brother die: "He was exactly one year old when he left this world. I was standing by his bed, crying. Mommy was simply looking. He seemed to understand. Mommy asked me not to cry, she said it made it more difficult for him to die. I squatted by the bedside, so that my little brother would not see me. Every now and then, I got up to look at him. Then mommy put a finger to her lips and I understood that my little brother was leaving us" (201–02). One additional reason for the sparsity of the prose is the simple fact that the narrators find it very difficult to speak of their experiences, the words are painful and speaking of these horrors means reliving them once more. It is likely, also, that not everything is told, by the women in particular, who will occasionally use the term "humiliation" or "degradation" without elaborating further.

Considering the endless suffering, the injustices, the tragic losses, and the wasted lives these narratives evoke, what is also striking is the calm resignation and the absence of hatred or of a desire for revenge that mark the concluding remarks made by the authors. Having recounted her work, which consisted of digging pits twenty feet deep and three feet wide in ground that was frozen solid, Veronika Goldmane concludes by asking, "How can you curse that place, where so much that remains has been built with my own hands? Where you have spent a good part of your youth, where so many tears have been shed, where I've experienced moments of joy, however brief?"[11] Speaking of the guards in her camp, Daina Smuldere-Gerke notes, "I do not want revenge. I can understand that they were cogs in an enormous mechanism" (237). She only sounds bitter when she considers that, today, her guards are probably enjoying all the privileges of the nomenclatura: the special hospitals, the special stores, and the choicest apartments. At the same time, the reader of these narratives cannot help but note that, while no revenge or retribution are demanded, a certain ironic literary justice is indeed achieved by them. On the one hand, the literature of deportation restores the humanity of those who were no longer considered human but who were mere numbers or, as they were known in some camps, humans of the second order. The guards, on the other hand, are annihilated; they are practically nonexistent; if they are evoked, it is only as anonymous, faceless figures, as the unthinking tools of a dehumanized and dehumanizing system.

The will to maintain a certain human dignity in the gulag, as the testimony of the victims makes clear, is often accompanied by an evocation of ancient, pre-Christian values and traditions. What emerges in this experience of an ethnic memory is an ethos that is specific to a certain Latvian cultural tradition. It is a philosophy of life harking back to a collective wisdom that is centuries-old and that has been preserved in the immensely rich and varied corpus of the *dainas* or folk songs.[12] Today, this legacy provides both a model and an opportunity for restoring a collective identity.

What is noteworthy about the cultural and religious ethos expressed by the *dainas*, is the contrast it offers with the Western axiological model. If we consider the notions of faith and reason, for example, concepts that are taken to be universals in the Western tradition, we find there is no distinction to be made between the two. From the perspective of the *dainas*, such categories as the "religious" or the "temporal," "faith" or "rationality" have no meaning. There are gods, but their existence does not require any special form of belief. Since there is no "faith," there is no need to impose it on anyone else. Consequently, there is no spiritual authority in which power is invested, no principle of supreme truth on the basis of which domination could be exercised. There is the recognition that other people may well think differently and have different beliefs, yet they are simply accepted for who they are and are considered neither better or worse, neither to be emulated nor converted.

The value system of the ancient Latvians, judging from the *dainas*, stands in complete contrast with the obsession to dominate nature and others, to dominate the Other—that could be considered a central tenet of the modern Western ethos since the time of Bacon and Descartes. Moreover, not only does it fail to elaborate any notion of cultural or ethnic superiority, the value system of the Letts even lacks what we would consider a commonsensical distinction between good and evil; there is suffering, there is misfortune, but there is no evil, no talk of vengeance, of retribution, or of damnation. Humans can be cruel and murderous, but that is because they are human and not because they are agents of darker forces. Even the enemy, in times of war, is more likely to be considered as a kindred spirit rather than someone to be hated.

In terms of positive values to live by, the principle that seems to dominate is that of the community, understood as a series of ever-expanding circles around the individual, who belongs to a family, an extended family, a county, a country, the world of humans, and the world of nature and the gods. The ties of love, respect, and obligation that bind the individual to these contexts are of utmost importance. A second major ethical principle is the importance of work. Work is the essence of a good life, it is the tie that binds the community and that gives meaning to existence. The ideal is thus to live a productive life in harmony with others and with nature.

One final distinction that opposes the world of the *dainas* to the ethos of the Western world needs to be mentioned. The cultural reality represented by the *dainas* is the work of women. In this sense, the worldview implicit in the conceptual universe of the *dainas* appears to hark back to an earlier, pre–Indo-European civilization not unlike the culture called "Old Europe" that has been characterized as "a culture matrifocal and probably matrilinear, agricultural and sedentary, egalitarian and peaceful"; it represents a perspective that stands opposed to "the ensuing proto–Indo-European culture which was patriarchal, stratified, pastoral, mobile, and war-oriented."[13] The fact that there were some fifty Mother-Goddesses in ancient Latvian folklore and mythology (Mother of Fire, of Water, of the Wind, etc.) is another indication of a tradition harking back to an earlier matrilinear cultural precedent. The *dainas* reflect then the sort of social arrangement in which women clearly enjoyed the dominating cultural role since it is evident that, in this society, the responsibility for composing, performing, and transmitting the *dainas* belonged to women. This task of giving a voice to a people's experience of life was not carried out by old men, by a priestly caste, or by an artistic or philosophic elite, as has been the case in all the so-called axial civilizations. It was a project that was fundamentally disinterested since it was both communal and anonymous.

In light of the ethical and cultural alternative implicit in the tradition of the *dainas*, the Western world of values appears both more and less imposing. On the one hand, a wisdom to be found in folklore, a folk song philosophy, might well appear rather paltry—laughable, even, next to the Western philosophical canon. On the other hand, unimposing though it might be, such an alternative worldview does make the Western ethos appear somewhat monolithic and uniform—even limited in its monotheistic, patriarchal, colonizing, capitalistic, and militaristic guises. And it does point out the arbitrariness of the West's pretense to universality. At the same time, if the Western ethos is obligated to recognize itself as simply one worldview among many, so does any other tradition—including that of the ancient Letts.

Any tradition, then, has to accept a dialectical obligation to balance an assertion of identity with a need for legitimization that can only be provided by others. This obligation becomes especially evident when justice is claimed in the name of human rights. A quest for recognition and for justice has to see itself as a fragment, as a part of a global striving. It cannot grant itself and by itself the coherence of a story with a beginning and a purpose; it is subject to a postmodern condition of our age because "our age lacks the structure of a story."[14] Yet, it is this very fragmentation of humanity's story that reintroduces the notion of universal concerns: "The fact that extremity can be translated the world over—that institutionalized suffering has been globalized—means that fragmentation might also be global—that displacement has been rendered universal."[15] Similarly, the quest for justice cannot proceed on the basis of claims made in the name of ethnic identity—it can only be carried out in the name of universal principles of humanity. It is an awareness that is especially evident in literatures of witnessing. As it establishes this link with humanity, a literature of witnessing both reinforces and justifies the specificity of ethnic identity. This is because the persuasiveness of any one call for justice becomes indebted to the other stories, the other fragments that belong to the genre that marks the tragic side of our century.

This newly formed identity is a product of history then, and represents a dialectical resolution of two opposing notions of identity that no longer appear to satisfy present requirements for understanding or defining human existence. It points to a newly created need to resolve the ages-old dichotomy of the particular and the universal bringing up, accordingly, the possibility of a new way of thinking the opposition. Ernesto Laclau sees this space as "an intellectual way opened by the very terrain in which History has thrown us: the multiplication of new—and not so new—identities as a result of the collapse of the places from which the universal subjects spoke."[16] The creation of this space is then a curious instance in which we see, as Laclau puts it, "the reemergence of the subject as a result of its own death; the proliferation of concrete finitudes whose limitations are the source of their strength; the realization that there can be 'subjects' because the gap that 'the subject' was supposed to bridge is actually unbridgeable" (94). It is the gap between the needs of concrete individuals and universal notions of humanity, between specific bodies and an imaginary social body. The history of this collapse is particularly revealing in the case of the failure of European Marxism to provide an identity that would reconcile individual needs with universal aspirations: "Between the universal character of the tasks of the working class and the particularity of its concrete demands, an increasing gap opened that had to be filled by the Party as the representative of the historical interests of the proletariat. The gap between class itself and class for itself opened the way to a succession of substitutions: the Party replaced the class, the autocrat the Party, and so on" (98). What Laclau provides in this brief outline is, in effect, the history of Stalinism and of its failed attempt at instituting a new form of humanity—*homo sovieticus*, to be exact. As the discrepancy between lived reality and utopian aspirations deepened, the gap became indeed unbridgeable; and while the project to erect *homo sovieticus* was meant to fulfill the philosophical quest initiated by Hegel and Marx, "who asserted the total transparency in absolute knowledge, of the real to reason" (97), it also demonstrated the project's impossibility. The contradiction implicit in this attempt to reconcile the universal with the particular was never to be resolved; it was a most telling example of a case, as Laclau notes, "in which social reality refused to abandon its resistance to universalistic rationalism" (97).

The gulag was the one place where this resistance became an integral part of the system—as its literature demonstrates. It was one place where the pretense of reconciling the particular with the universal was nullified, by definition, because inmates no longer belonged to the category of the human. From the prisoners' perspective, it was the one place where truth emerged following the disintegration of the pretense that *homo sovieticus* had represented. It was a truth that explained the martyrization of millions and justified any remaining resolve to survive—the only value worth clinging to—the truth of one's ethnicity or nationality. As Forché points out, "Where Stalin erased the past and the present for the supposed good of the future, the poet asks the past and the present to stake a claim on that future."[17]

While this claim on the future made in the name of a past and a present effectively legitimates a concern for the universal, as we have seen, it also calls for a new and different understanding of the universal. It is now evident, for example, that the universal and the particular are by no means contradictory or mutually exclusive notions. As Gregory Bruce Smith suggests, "We must be open to both the universal and the particular, identity and difference, unity and diversity. These are either/or choices only within a modern perspective."[18] Thus, an ethnic or national identity that asserts itself in terms of its own immanence makes no sense, because, as Laclau points out, "The assertion of pure particularism, independently of any content and of the appeal to a universality transcending it, is a self-defeating enterprise" (99). Moreover, as sociologists have shown, individual experience has no meaning in and of itself: "Even if experience is considered, more often than not, as being purely individual, it is still true that it truly exists in the eyes of the individual only to the extent that it is recognized by others, especially when it is shared and confirmed by others."[19] To put the same idea philosophically, the universal is necessary because it is what is lacking in a particular identity; the latter is indeed constituted by this very lack; the universal "is part of my identity as far as I am penetrated by a constitutive lack" (101).

The dialectical relation between the universal and the particular has important implications for the resolution of relations of domination and oppression. When oppression is lifted in a society, it becomes important not to simply reverse the situation of domination. In this regard, Laclau finds instructive the reasoning of a South African friend of his, Aletta Norval, who finds it essential that the relationship between dominators and dominated not simply be reversed and the form of repression not be retained in a postapartheid South Africa. She therefore deems it imperative to preserve the memory of apartheid: "Through a remembrance of apartheid as other, post-apartheid could become the site from which the final closure and suturing of identities is to be prevented. Paradoxically, a post-apartheid society will then only be radically beyond apartheid in so far as apartheid itself is present in it as its other" (103). Thus the universal is prevented from becoming a totalitarian pretense because it is counterbalanced by the memory of the particular instance of oppression. The former victims have to realize that the universal requirement of humanity and justice to which they appealed is not annulled but has acquired even greater legitimacy and relevance following the elimination of oppression. If they were to reinstitute oppression, the victims would be promoting their particularism to the level of the absolute or the universal, thus effectively canceling the latter. And, simultaneously, their own position would thereby turn self-referential, thus vacuous. As Laclau explains it, the strategy suggested by Norval consists of attacking the universal pretense that legitimated oppression; it is a tactic that ends up, "instead of inverting a particular relation of oppression/closure in what it has of concrete particularity, inverting it in what it has of universality: the *form* of oppression and closure as such. The reference to the other is maintained here also, but as the inversion takes place at the level of the universal reference and not of the concrete contents of an oppressive system, the identities of *both* oppressors and oppressed are radically changed" (104). Consequently, an effective strategy of resistance will seek to transform the very logic of the system that makes oppression possible and be predicated on the understanding that "a system of oppression (i.e., of closure) can be combated in two different ways—either by an operation of inversion which performs a new closure, or by negating in that system its universal dimension: the principle of closure as such" (106).

Gulag literature provides a remarkable illustration of this wisdom. The authors do not write to express a desire for retribution or to seek vengeance. The camp guards, for example, when they appear in the narratives, are not presented as objects of the inmates' hatred. What surfaces instead, is a desire to maintain humanity, even a certain human dignity in the face of bestial behavior and utterly demeaning conditions. This dignity is often preserved as a sense of identity gained in a movement of solidarity toward the other victims, the other inmates. It is as if the inmates of the gulag were able to rise to a higher state of awareness that made them understand the truth of the necessary relationship between their particular suffering and the universal requirement of compassion. It is a state that made them realize that the concrete experience of victimhood cannot, in turn, become a universal motive for retribution—for then the universal would be annihilated. There is no satisfying solution, then, to the situation of the victim, no restitution to compensate for the losses incurred. However, as Laclau points out, it is the acceptance of this nonsolution that "is the very precondition of democracy," because it "burdens concrete social agents with that impossible task that makes democratic interaction achievable" (107). It is a burden symptomatic of our times, perhaps, and is thus to be seen as yet another fragment of a more general undertaking—which is the equally daunting task of reconstructing a reason for our age.

Epilogue

Once we accept the proposition—implicit in a number of post-modern critiques—that modernity is floundering because of defects and contradictions inherent in its very constitution, we can understand why the reasons for modernity's failure to fulfill its promise are to be found in the very form this promise has taken. The appeal of the promise was so strong that it sustained for a long time an unshakable belief in what were, after all, nothing more than imaginary constructs. Such beliefs usually made it difficult to accept the possibility that the world might not operate according to the tenets promoted by various theoretical constructions, that history might not follow the plan that seemed so natural and normal to a Western mind. Foucault draws a distinction between "effective" history and history as it has been conceived traditionally—in terms of unifying themes and causality, and notes that "'effective' history differs from traditional history in being without constants. Nothing in man—not even his body—is sufficiently stable to serve as the basis for self-recognition or for understanding other men."[1] It was to cover up this deficiency that humanisms of various sorts needed to be constructed. A human essence, a telos for humanity needed to be posited in order to provide rationalizations for programs aspiring to improve the lot of humanity. Once the rationales were in place, the application of power could proceed according to the interests of those holding it. Thus the phantasms of modernity's promises not only occluded systems of domination but entered into collusion with them by providing admirable motives for ignoble designs.

But the contradiction sustaining the pretense also worked to undermine it. Thus the Soviet experiment eventually unraveled because the contrast between the official version and the evidence at hand simply became untenable. The demise of the Soviet Union was of course greeted with a great deal of self-congratulatory satisfaction in the West.[2] With the enemy gone, however, the Western socioeconomic model has been required to justify itself strictly in terms of its own merits and it is becoming apparent that the disappearance of the Red Menace has also eliminated what was, for the First World, a very useful alibi. Now that it stands alone, the ideology of the victorious side has become increasingly questionable and Capitalism's promise of a better life and greater social justice for all of humanity is itself beginning to display the tell-tale characteristics of a vast pretense. Which is to say that the pretense is rapidly losing its credibility.

The point at which it unravels most visibly is in the claim that the interests of capitalist enterprise and the cause of social progress coincide. One strategy used to sustain the claim has been to marshal certain ideals, such as the notion of freedom, in the service of economic interests. As one of the key principles in the Western ethos, freedom offers the distinct advantage of rendering unimpeachable any claim made in its name. Business interests have therefore exploited fully the advantages of this association. Thus, not too long ago, a major oil company ran the following ad on television: "Freedom is our most important resource," it proposed. "It should never be governed away. Something to think about. From the people at Getty."

Now, obviously, the people at Getty were also hoping that viewers would not think too long about their slogan but be moved, instead, to instinctively identify the oil business with freedom and government interference with tyranny. Because slogans can effectively block the process of serious thinking, tactics exemplified by the Getty ad have been eminently successful in this country—especially in the political arena. In coopting the rhetoric of democracy and freedom, business interests appear to be well on their way to making the political decision-making process largely irrelevant or, to be more accurate, into a pretense whose purpose is mainly to shield the workings of the market system. This is the conclusion William Greider reaches in his eye-opening study of the global economic situation. Greider finds that political thinking in the West is so hopelessly outmoded that it is no longer relevant to what is happening in the world today; as a result, "the logic of commerce and capital have overpowered the inertia of politics and launched an epoch of great social transformations."[3] The logic and direction of changes taking place—as befits any system operating behind a pretense—are no longer affected by the official ideology. It is a disjuncture particularly evident in the case of one of the most commonly used alibis—the alleged freedom of the market.

As Greider effectively demonstrates, the notion of a free market turns out to be a sham in several respects. In the first place, there never has been any such thing: "Despite the reigning pieties, the global system could not properly be called a free-trade regime. When all of the contradictions, exceptions and purposeful evasions were taken into account, most of the world's trade was not a free exchange based on market prices. One way or another, trade was massaged and regulated, managed explicitly by governments or internally by the multinational corporations or often by both in discreet collaboration."[4] Second, it is also clear that freedom, as such, is a condition that goes counter to the best interests of multinational corporations, and while capitalism "claims to promote human freedom, it profits from the denial of freedom."[5] The efficiency of business operations is enhanced by a strictly regimented and exploitative workplace. As a result, the principles of freedom or equity find themselves systematically abrogated by business practices across the globe. The pretense has been equally useful in the United States, where an uncritical adherence to an obsolescent ideological discourse has been the necessary element in the perpetuation of existing conditions of socioeconomic selection and promotion. The pro–free-market propaganda campaign has been able to go on largely unchallenged here, because "mainstream political perspectives were blinkered to the larger failure of the marketplace—the existing universe of work and incomes that effectively guaranteed that gross inequalities, disappointment and even cruel deprivation would continue to accumulate in the wealthiest nation on earth."[6]

What helps keep the pretense in place in the United States, is also a culturally ingrained predisposition to find disparities in wealth as natural, if not divinely ordained. It is a perspective deriving from various themes of individual agency and responsibility—a vague amalgam of a Cartesian-Kantian thesis of subjective autonomy combined with the Protestant theme of personal redemption and responsibility. In this context, the union between reason and virtue becomes axiomatic. As a consequence, the two methods deemed most useful for regulating social existence are indoctrination and punishment: to ensure order and progress, virtue must be taught and infractions to the moral and legal codes must be punished. The twin themes of family values and state-enacted retribution are familiar rhetorical devices for politicians eager to be identified with correct thought in these matters. Books on virtue become bestsellers; state appropriations for the construction of prisons are breaking all records, legislation promoting ever-harsher sentences and more speedy applications of the death penalty is underwritten and applauded by the self-righteous of both major political persuasions.

The constant appeal to moral values also serves a most significant purpose, never acknowledged by the promoters of justice based on morality: it clears the defenders of law and order of any accountability for the plight of the have-nots by making the wretched of society morally responsible for their condition.[7] Victims of economic downturns, of "downsizings," or other negative effects of the marketplace have been typically prone to blame themselves, as Greider notes, since "the culture of individualism did not prepare people to understand the failure as systemic, not personal."[8] Generally speaking then, the system seems well designed to ensure a clear conscience for the well-off in terms of the prevalent moral and religious standards. As added insurance, it is also helpful to identify villains—to blame, for example, certain cultural trends or to demonize vague institutionalized "systems" such as the "government," the "entertainment industry," the "liberal press," and the "leftist university."

Such arguments help deflect attention from the socioeconomic inequities that affect lives in very real, tangible, material ways. But they are also becoming transparent. As Lester Thurow reminds us: "The traditional family is being destroyed not by misguided social welfare programs coming from Washington . . . but by a modern economic system that is not congruent with 'family values.'"[9] The discourse of moral values becomes particularly cynical when it serves to ease society's conscience in regard to the deteriorating conditions of existence for children in the United States; thus Katherine Paterson points to an obvious but telling evidence: "In the present climate we seem to be teaching [the children] that values are something the rich and the powerful offer the poor and weak instead of adequate nutrition, health care, good schools, job training and an equal opportunity for life, liberty and the pursuit of happiness."[10]

Implicit in such commentaries aiming to disclose the hypocrisy underlying ways of rationalizing our society's more dysfunctional aspects, is the understanding that the culturally ingrained notion of the individual's capacity and responsibility is fundamentally flawed. The belief in an individual's ability to mold and control the real is increasingly contradicted by the evidence of the effect the global marketplace is having on human relationships. For one thing, in its relentless promotion of uniform modes of entertainment and consumption, the global market is effectively breaking up existing ties that bind individuals to local communities and traditions. In addition, capitalism remains highly immature as a social system, because, as Greider shows, "The capitalist process, by its nature, encourages infantile responses from every quarter, as people are led to maximize self-interest and evade responsibility for the collateral consequences of their activities, the damage to other people or society or the natural environment."[11]

The Cartesian-Kantian theme of individual agency and its promise of an effective rationalization and, consequently, of an assured domination of reality can, in this light, only appear as a pretense to be discarded. As Georgia Warnke notes, for example, what makes Kantian approaches to political philosophy defective is that "they seem to ignore the rich, lived-in character of the principles and practices a community may already possess."[12] Moreover, the obsessive tendency to effectuate domination over the world, over its peoples and over nature, can have and has often had a contradictory effect. As Régis Debray reminds us, a promise of mastery over reality can legitimate the irrational once more, since "the more the world is mastered and modeled, the more its objective reality becomes blurred and estranged from its users. At the end of modernity, we find God and the Devil again—and the priests."[13]

A distinguishing trait of postmodernists, as we have seen, is the refusal to place themselves outside or above the real: they understand themselves thoroughly implicated in a "reality" that they are themselves—but that is largely constituted outside and in spite of themselves. As the sense that modernity tried to make of the world disintegrates, we are reminded anew that our thinking, seeing, representing do not "reproduce" or "copy" reality. Rather, as Nancy suggests, "We could say that it is something more like 'recording': entering in an order of markings a reality that is heterogenous to this order and does not become homogenous with it."[14] It is a process, moreover, that relies on interpretation. Because interpretation has always had such a crucial role in Western modes of cogitation it has also come to signify Western culture's disenchantment and exhaustion. And for cause: once interpretation is acknowledged as the inseparable component of thinking it serves as a constant reminder of the incompleteness of knowledge and the impossibility of ever finding a secure basis for values or principles that would guide our actions.

It is an insecurity that many find intolerable today and that gives rise to reactive and reactionary movements for restoring certain knowledge and correct thinking. As familiar and comforting political and religious convictions dissipate, there resound calls for the reaffirmation of bygone certitudes. As Nancy puts it: "Precipitous, fearful, and reactive thinking consists today in declaring as indispensable the most ordinarily recognizable forms of identification, forms that their own destinies have used up or perverted: 'people,' 'nation,' 'church,' 'culture,' to say nothing of the confusing 'ethnicity,' nor of the twisted 'roots.'"

To make such references valid once more, however, requires a capacity to deny the tectonic shift that has taken place in Western culture and thought over the last decades of this century. The shift manifests itself as a radical modification in our ways of thinking about thought and about its capacity for determining truth and imposing identity. In light of these transformations, an appeal to essences can only appear futile because today, any mode of self-representation and self-legitimization refers back, not "to an origin, but to the hollowness of its own specularity."[15] No singular claim of truth or value derived from a notion of identity can maintain itself; it should be evident, explains Nancy, that if any notion of the "human" has any worth, then it can only be in relation to a "*plurality* which singularity implies as does the notion of 'worth' itself: for indeed, what could possibly be worth anything for itself, except itself? Worth can only have value in an order of being with, that is in an order of *commerce* in every sense of the word." An identity promoting itself in terms of its own worth is nothing more than a vestige of modernity's propensity for valorizing itself on the basis of the definition it generates for itself; it is a tactic exemplified by "the impasse reached by Kant, and perpetuated by Hegel, that universal Reason exists as an *a priori* phenomenon, self-referential and grounded in itself."[16]

The increasingly persistent manifestation of this impasse also suggests that it has become possible to elaborate new modes of thought. Thus Le Doeuff proposes that "it is possible to think of rationality otherwise than in a hegemonic mode."[17] It is therefore important to discard the remaining pretenses that maintained the hegemonic mode because "it is now possible to cease wishing to mask the incomplete nature of all theorization." What such a rejection requires is the maturity to understand the paradoxical nature of knowledge and to accept that "Knowledge is always defective, but nevertheless still a necessity."[18]

It is equally necessary to understand that the quest for knowledge is an interminable process. And although it may appear at times that nothing essentially new or different can be said about the human condition, the obverse is also true, as Nancy reminds us: "Everything has been said, to be sure, because everything has always already been said, but everything is still to be said, because the whole as such needs always to be said anew."[19] What has changed is the ambition to rationalize and change the whole. There are still those who claim to possess the truth and who would have everyone submit to it. But we have also good reasons for valuing skepticism in such matters. I much prefer, said Foucault, "the very precise transformations that have taken place in the last twenty years in a certain number of domains that concern modes of being and of thinking, relations of authority, relations between sexes, the way in which we perceive madness or illness. I prefer even these partial changes that have been made in the correlation of historical analysis with practical attitudes, to the promises a new humanity that the worst political systems have reiterated along the twentieth century."[20] We have seemingly come to a moment in history when it is time once more, in Nietzsche's words, to "give the earth a meaning, a human meaning."[21] It is a time when the partial, the local, the concrete, and the contingent appear to emerge once more as values that will give shape to a new opportunity for rethinking our world and ourselves.

What emerges as well, is a record of human experience that modernity had suppressed or deemed irrelevant. One such area concerns the part women have played in the history of civilizations. It is a neglect that is beginning to be remedied, as Gerda Lerner explains:

> Women have always lived in history, acted in it and made history. But the history of women was, up until about thirty years ago, distorted in peculiar way: it came

to us refracted through the lens of male observation and distorted through an interpretation based on patriarchal values. The new women's history has undertaken the task of reconstructing the missing half and of putting women as active agents in the center of events in order that recorded history might at last reflect the dual nature of humankind in its true balance, its female and its male aspects.[22]

To be sure, the patriarchal bias is not characteristic of modernity alone and, at least in this regard, modernity was not at all modern but simply enshrined in its own way (often in the name of reason, as we have seen), a prejudice already ages-old. Other exclusionary practices, however, can be considered as integral parts of the very strategy that ensured modernity's successful reign. Thus a low regard for history and tradition complemented its future orientation and was a necessary component of its campaign to establish the autonomous and self-validating position of reason. From a philosophical perspective, the tactic produced certain characteristic aspects that were eventually to prove largely debilitating.

First, the reliance on the highly abstract powers and prerogatives of reason led to an obsessive concern with introspective ratiocination. As a result, as we see from John Deely's study of a philosophic tradition effectively suppressed by modernity, the procedure constituting modernity was, from its very beginnings, remarkably reductive in its effects because "the moderns reduced philosophy's concerns to what was supposed to be distinctively rational or natural in the context of the mind's workings."[23] It was a procedure that elided the existential and experiential context for thought by failing to take into account thought's hermeneutical mode of functioning—that is, by refusing to see that thinking is always/already epistemologically and ontologically grounded in a context that preconditions understanding. Descartes, as Deely shows, had a key role to play in this regard, and "the general prejudice [he] engendered against the importance of history for the philosopher" was to have profound consequences.[24] Specifically, the prejudice had the effect of occluding a long and rich tradition of late Latin and early modern Hispanic philosophic thought, a history that turns out to be of particular interest for us today because some of its themes resonate in striking ways with postmodern concerns. It appears then that "the modern paradigm was so formed as to conceal from the outset fundamental themes of premodern Latin thought which are, in effect, resumed and foregrounded (with new accents and emphases, to be sure) by the postmodern development."[25]

Second, over time, the claim of reason's absolute status and universal applicability gradually blended with assertions of geopolitical infallibility. Thus modernity's hegemonic expansion was accomplished in tandem with the assertion of the universality of Western values and the mission to civilize others became a humanitarian pursuit. The thought and traditions of other cultures could therefore be no more than simply "other," and remain forever marked by a seemingly insuperable relation of dependency—even after the departure of the colonizers.

Africans, for example, have found it particularly difficult to escape the cultural subjection imposed on them by the binary opposition implicit in their postcolonial status. They find themselves relegated to dependency whenever considerations of African culture and history are drawn into a debate governed by the paradigmatic categories of Western modernity—whenever the debate revolves around such themes as Rationality, Art, Culture, Science, or Technology. So long as modernity continues to dictate the criteria for civilized achievement, Africans are condemned in advance in terms of one or another version of "the broken promise of modernity" leitmotif. As Achille Mbembe explains, African writers and thinkers have constantly found themselves caught in "an intellectual tragedy of a specific sort, whereby all discourse on Africa is obliged to inscribe itself in a horizon dominated by a single legitimate problematic: why a movement similar to that which resulted in the emergence of what one calls Western 'modernity' did not take place here?"[26] The crucial task has therefore been to find ways of protecting the difference of the "other" in the face of a modernity that imposes itself culturally and economically as the universal standard and to avoid being assimilated "as an inferior, subordinate and exploited term, . . . a mere inversion, a mere Calibanic counterdiscourse."[27] It is a question of ensuring the survival of a cultural legacy, of valorizing "a desire, a will to tap into memories and energies encoded in oral traditions and the pre-colonial cultural ensembles that face the threat of obliteration by a colonizing modernity, a *capitalist* homogenizing modernity."[28]

What makes resistance possible today is the awareness of modernity's vulnerability, the realization that its gradual disintegration is under way and can even be speeded up by "the arduous task of unpacking the racial, cultural, class, gender and individual myths intricately lodged at the heart of virtually all discourses of modernity and its discontents."[29] It is a task taking place neither in terms of the "same" or the "other" but in a space separating the two. African authors have thus been able, not only to enrich the borrowed languages of a European literary tradition with local materials, with the inherited languages of tradition and myth: they have also opened up the perspective of a third dimension by couching their narratives in "the new languages of contemporary life, politics, and intellectual thought." And while these are languages that frequently clash with the established idioms of literary representation, "it is in these tensions that the novelist mediates in a narrative that is very much centered in the contemporary realities of Africa."[30] Instead of asserting certitudes and values, these texts problematize them; rather than being dependent on Eurocentric thinking, African literature has developed a capacity for destabilizing the ways of establishing knowledge and ratifying truths instituted by the West. Once the criteria set by modernity are no longer admitted for purposes of judging or suppressing the past, what stands out are the narrow limits set by a discourse of modernity, as well as the self-serving poverty of modernity's own conceptual scope and imagination.

The tables thus suddenly find themselves turned: it is modernity that is made to appear as a localized system of thought whose persuasiveness is mainly attributable to the economic and military superiority of the West and not to the allegedly self-evident truths of its political and religious discourses. In 1956, on the occasion of the first "World Conference of Negro Men of Culture" in Paris, Alioune Diop was calling into question all those "eminent men of culture" whose pronouncements "make it clearly understood that only the West can aspire to be regarded as having the right to be universal."[31] Today the mythical pretense through which the West has been able to attribute to itself the capacity for legislating globally what is rational, moral, and normal has imploded. In the void that is left, new forms of thinking and writing are free to organize.

In this regard, the debates revolving around African literatures can be seen to belong to a more general movement of ideas whose purpose has been to bring into question established modes of thought. It is therefore inevitable, as Eileen Julien notes, that African texts be "read as a part of a vast movement of postcolonial writing, which, in tandem with poststructuralism and feminism, has been a powerful force in the Western academy's recognition of Literature's embeddedness in social and political practices and consequently in the interrogation of the very idea of 'the West.'"[32] It is an interrogation directed at what Nana Wilson-Tagoe calls a monocentric view of reality. Indeed, she finds there is reason to believe that an African skeptical turn preceded the postmodern one, suggesting that "it can be argued further that the post-colonial writer's dismantling of a monocentric view of reality and culture through his/her subjective representation of another reality preceded the post-structuralist attack on assumptions about language and textuality. There is then a certain intersection between post-colonial theory and post-modernist theory."[33]

The nature and destiny modernity attempted to devise for humanity turn out to have been illusions. As these pretenses fade and dissipate, we become increasingly aware that our time is taking shape in ways yet unforeseen and not yet comprehensible. It is an awareness to be cultivated. As Mbembe notes, "I am simply trying to read and write Africa from a rift." Consequently, "It is legitimate to explore the hypothesis that another epoch, another temporality is at work. One can call it the postcolony, or not. That is not really the question."[34] Similarly, whether we call our time postmodern or not, it clearly offers a vantage that distances us from modernity and its convictions, making us receptive to the disclosures of a changing reality. What we make of this experience will determine the validity of a thought still being elaborated and will, hopefully, inspire rather than perplex future analysts of these circumstances.

Notes

INTRODUCTION

1. Max Oelschlager, "Introduction," in *Postmodern Environmental Ethics*, ed. Max Oelschlager (Albany: SUNY Press, 1995), 2.

2. Zygmunt Bauman, *Modernity and Ambivalence* (Cambridge: Polity Press, 1991), 7.

3. D. H. Lawrence, "Chaos in Poetry," in *Selected Literary Criticism*, ed. Anthony Bell (Melbourne, London, Toronto: Heinemann Ltd., 1955), 90.

4. Ibid.

5. Ibid., 91–92.

6. Stephen Dobyns, *The Wrestler's Cruel Study* (New York: W. W. Norton, 1993), 286–87.

7. Jean-Luc Nancy, *L'oubli de la philosophie* (Paris: Galilée, 1986), 66. All translations of French texts are mine.

8. Jean-Luc Nancy, *Etre singulier pluriel* (Paris: Galilée, 1996), 12.

9. Ibid., 11.

10. Nancy, *L'oubli de la philosophie*, 71.

11. Ibid., 99–100.

12. Nancy, *Etre singulier pluriel*, 20.

13. Gordon Globus, *The Postmodern Brain* (Amsterdam and Philadelphia: John Benjamins, 1995), 127.

14. Ibid., 131.

15. Ibid., 130.

16. Michel Foucault, *L'ordre du discours* (Paris: Galillimard, 1971), 74.

17. Ernst Cassirer, *Symbol, Myth, and Culture: Essays and Lectures of Ernst Cassirer, 1935–1945*, ed. Donald Phillip Verene (New Haven: Yale Univ. Press, 1979), 62.

18. Murray Code, *Myths of Reason* (Atlantic Highlands, N.J.: Humanities Press, 1996), ix.

19. Todd May, *The Moral Theory of Poststructuralism* (University Park, PA: The Pennsylvania State Univ. Press, 1995), 70–71.

20. Code, *Myths of Reason*, 11 and 9.

21. Bauman, *Modernity and Ambivalence*, 232.

22. Ibid., 29.

23. John Ralston Saul, *Voltaire's Bastards: The Dictatorship of Reason in the West* (New York: Free Press, 1992), 20.

24. Arthur Schopenhauer, *On the Basis of Morality* (Indianapolis: Bobbs-Merrill, 1965), 83.

25. Susan R. Bordo, *The Flight to Objectivity: Essays on Cartesianism and Culture* (New York: SUNY Press, 1987), 17.

26. Code, *Myths of Reason*, 111.

27. Milton K. Munitz, *The Question of Reality* (Princeton: Princeton Univ. Press, 1990), 105.

28. Edo Pivcevic, *The Concept of Reality* (London: Duckworth, 1986), 275.

29. Ibid., 284.

30. Munitz, *The Question of Reality*, 130.

31. Code, *Myths of Reason*, x.

32. Ibid., 56.

33. Ibid., 116.

34. Ibid., 73.

35. Owen Barfield, *Saving the Appearances: A Study in idolatry* (London: Faber and Faber, 1965), 20.

36. Ibid., 118.

37. Ibid., 60.

38. Ibid., 117.

39. Owen Barfield, *Speaker's Meaning* (Middletown, Conn.: Wesleyan Univ. Press, 1967), 105.

40. Code, *Myths of Reason*, 69.

41. Ibid., 90.

42. Ibid., 122.

43. Adam Schaff, "Vague Words," in *Semiotics in Poland*, ed. Jerzy Pelc (Warsaw: Polish Scientific Publishers, 1979), 236.

44. Roland Barthes, *Critique et vérité* (Paris: Seuil, 1966), 51.

45. Code, *Myths of Reason*, 102.

46. Ibid., 217.

47. May, *The Moral Theory of Poststructuralism*, 71.

48. François Dubet, *Sociologie de l'expérience* (Paris: Seuil, 1994), 55.

49. Ibid., 16.

50. Ibid., 94. It is an idea akin to Pierre Bourdieu's notion of *habitus*, a term used to designate a socially and culturally ingrained predisposition that gives our ways of knowing and behaving the appearance of naturalness. As Bourdieu explains it: "The schemes of the habitus, the primary forms of classification, owe their specific efficacy to the fact that they function below the level of consciousness and language, beyond the reach of introspective scrutiny or control by the will." Pierre Bourdieu, *Distinction: A Social Critique of the Judgement of Taste* (Cambridge, Mass.: Harvard Univ. Press, 1984), 466.

51. Ibid., 108.

52. Ibid., 103.

53. Ibid., 133.

54. Ibid., 255.

55. Ibid., 254.

56. Charles Siebert, "The DNA We've Been Dealt," *New York Times Magazine*, 17 Sept. 1995, 104.

57. David R. Hiley, *Philosophy in Question: Essays on a Pyrrhonian Theme* (Chicago: The Univ. of Chicago Press, 1988), 14–15.

58. As I have already argued in *Postmodernism and the Search for Enlightenment* (Charlottesville: The Univ. Press of Virginia, 1993). See Chapter 6, "Candide's Garden Revisited: The Postmodern View."

59. Barry Allen, *Truth in Philosophy* (Cambridge, Mass.: Harvard Univ. Press, 1993), 111.

60. Bordo, *The Flight to Objectivity*, 117.

61. Genevieve Lloyd, *The Man of Reason: "Male" and "Female" in Western Philosophy* (Minneapolis: Univ. of Minnesota Press, 1993), 49.

62. Ibid., 49–50.

63. Lawrence E. Cahoone, *The Dilemma of Modernity: Philosophy, Culture, and Anti-Culture* (Albany: SUNY Press, 1988), 74.

64. The Constitution of the USSR is very explicit, in this regard. It guaranteed its citizens "political freedoms—freedom of

speech, the press, assembly, meetings, street processions, and demonstrations." It granted them political rights: "the right to participate in the administration of state and public affairs, to make proposals to state and public organizations concerning ways to improve their activity, to criticize shortcomings on the job, to associate in public organizations, and to vote." It enumerated "personal rights and freedoms" that included "the inviolability of the individual and of the home, freedom of conscience, the right to legal defense, and the right to lodge complaints concerning the actions of officials and state and public organs." It stipulated that "the personal lives of citizens and privacy of correspondence, telephone conversations, and telegraph communications are protected by law." It made clear that all these rights "are granted to all citizens regardless of origin, social or property status, race or nationality, sex, education, language, attitude to religion, type or nature of occupation, domicile or other status." And it declared that "women and men have equal rights." *Great Soviet Encyclopedia*, 3d ed. (New York: Macmillan, 1979), vol. 13, p. 574.

1. VOLTAIRE AND THE LIMITS OF REASON

1. Hiley, *Philosophy in Question*, 63.

2. Lawrence E. Cahoone, *The Dilemma of Modernity: Philosophy, Culture, and Anti-Culture* (Albany: SUNY Press, 1988), xv.

3. In *Postmodernism and the Search for Enlightenment.*

4. Voltaire, *The Philosophy of History*, in *The Complete Romances of Voltaire. Also The Philosophy of History, The Ignorant Philosopher, Dialogues and Philosophic Criticisms* (New York: Walter J. Black Co., 1927), 386. Translation slightly modified.

5. Didier Masseau, "Raison," in *Inventaire Voltaire*, ed. Jean Goulemont, André Magnan, Didier Masseau (Paris: Gallimard, 1995), 1139.

6. Page numbers for quotations refer to René Pomeau's edition of Voltaire's *Romans et Contes* (Paris: Garnier-Flammarion, 1966). The translations are mine.

7. Voltaire, *Dictionnaire Philosophique* (Amsterdam: Marc-Michel Rey, 1789), vol. vi, p. 451.

8. Hans-Georg Gadamer, *Truth and Method*, xxiii.

9. Paul Ricoeur, *The Conflict of Interpretations*, ed. Don Ihde (Evanston: Northwestern Univ. Press, 1974), 66.

10. Ibid., 401.

11. John Ralston Saul, *Voltaire's Bastards*, 17.

12. Luc Brisson and F. Walter Meyerstein, *Puissance et limites de la raison: Le problème des valeurs* (Paris: Les Belles Lettres, 1995), 11.

13. Joan Stambaugh, *The Real Is Not the Rational* (Albany: SUNY Press, 1986), ix.

2. THE POSTMODERN OUTLOOK FOR HERMENEUTICS

1. Gayle L. Ormiston and Alan D. Schrift, "Editor's Introduction," in *The Hermeneutic Tradition: From Ast to Ricoeur* (Albany: SUNY Press, 1990), 2.

2. Jean Starobinski, *Montaigne in Motion*, trans. Arthur Goldhammer (Chicago: Univ. of Chicago Press, 1985), 27.

3. Gayle L. Ormiston and Alan D. Schrift, "Editor's Introduction," in *Transforming the Hermeneutic Context: From Nietzsche to Nancy* (Albany: SUNY Press, 1990), 5.

4. Ibid.

5. Friedrich D. E. Schleiermacher, "The Aphorisms on Hermeneutics from 1805 and 1809/10," in *The Hermeneutic Tradition*, 76.

6. Friedrich D. E. Schleiermacher, "The Hermeneutics: Outline of the 1819 Lectures," in *The Hermeneutic Tradition*, 85.

7. Martin Heidegger, "*Being and Time*: Sections 31–34," in *The hermeneutic Tradition*, 121.

8. Ibid., 122.

9. Ibid., 125.

10. Ibid., 126.

11. Ibid., 134.

12. Hans-Georg Gadamer, "The Universality of the Hermeneutical Problem," in *The Hermeneutic Tradition*, 151.

13. Ibid., 152.

14. Hans-Georg Gadamer, "*Truth and Method*: 'Introduction' and 'Foreword to the Second Edition,'" in *The Hermeneutic Tradition*, 200–01.

15. Ibid., 200.

16. Ibid., 205.

17. Paul Ricoeur, "Hermeneutics and the Critique of Ideology," in *The Hermeneutic Tradition*, 321.

18. Ibid., 313.

19. Ibid., 330.

20. Charles E. Scott, *The Question of Ethics: Nietzsche, Foucault, Heidegger* (Bloomington: Indiana Univ. Press, 1990), 62.

21. Ibid.

22. Ormiston and Schrift, "Editor's Introduction," in *The Hermeneutic Tradition*, 28.

23. Michel Foucault, "Nietzsche, Freud, Marx," in *Transforming the Hermeneutic Context*, 59.

24. Julia Kristeva, "Psychoanalysis and the Polis," in *Transforming the Hermeneutic Context*, 90.

25. Jean-Luc Nancy, "Sharing Voices," in *Transforming the Hermeneutic Context*, 212.

26. Richard A. Cohen, "Absolute Positivity and Ultrapositivity: Husserl and Levinas," in *The Question of the Other: Essays in Contemporary Continental Philosophy*, ed. Arleen B. Dallery and Charles E. Scott (Albany: SUNY Press, 1989), 40.

27. Ibid., 39–40.

28. Adriaan Peperzak, "From Intentionality to Responsibility: On Levinas's Philosophy of Language," in *The Question of the Other*, 19.

29. Cohen, "Absolute Positivity and Ultrapositivity," 41.

30. Peperzak, "From Intentionality to Responsibility," 20.

31. Robert Bernasconi, "Rereading *Totality and Infinity*," in *The Question of the Other*, 31–32.

32. Cohen, "Absolute Positivity and Ultrapositivity," 41.

33. Diane Michelfelder, "Derrida and the Ethics of the Ear," in *The Question of the Other*, 52.

34. Ibid., 52–53.

35. Michael D. Barber, "Alma Gonzalez: Otherness as Attending to the Other," in *The Question of the Other*, 124.

36. Kenneth Liberman, "Decentering the Self: Two Perspectives from Philosophical Anthropology," in *The Question of the Other*, 132.

37. Ibid., 142.

38. Ibid., 132.

39. Ibid., 139.

40. Ladelle McWhorter, "Foucault's Analytics of Power," in *Crises in Continental Philosophy*, ed. Arleen B. Dallery and Charles E. Scott, with P. Holley Roberts (Albany: SUNY Press, 1990), 126.

41. David F. Gruber, "Foucault and Theory: Genealogical Critiques of the Subject," in *The Question of the Other*, 192.

42. McWhorter, "Foucault's Analytics of Power," 123.

43. Linda Singer, "Defusing the Canon: Feminist Rereading and Textual Politics," in *The Question of the Other*, 107.

44. Ibid.

45. Ibid., 112.

46. Dennis J. Schmidt, "Economies of Production: Heidegger and Aristotle on *Physis* and *Technè*," in *Crises in Continental Philosophy*, 148.

47. Gayle L. Ormiston, "Postmodern *différends*," in *Crises in Continental Philosophy*, 235.

48. Ibid., 237.

49. Ibid., 244.

50. McWhorter, "Foucault's Analytics of Power," 125.

51. Thomas R. Thorp, "Derrida and Habermas on the Subject of Political Philosophy," in *Crises in Continental Philosophy*, 87.

52. Ibid., 89.

53. Liberman, "Decentering the Self," 132.

54. Hans-Georg Gadamer, "Foreword," in Jean Grondin, *L'universalité de l'herméneutique* (Paris: PUF, 1993), vi.

55. Ibid., ix.

56. Ibid., vi.

57. Ibid., 162.

58. Ibid., 37.

59. Ibid.

60. Ibid., 164.

61. Ibid., 127.

62. Ibid., 137.

63. Schleiermacher, "The Hermeneutics," 86.

64. Ormiston, "Postmodern *différends*," 245.

3. MICHÈLE LE DOEUFF'S PHILOSOPHY OF DISINVOLVEMENT

1. Michèle Le Doeuff, *Hipparchia's Choice: An Essay Concerning Women, Philosophy, Etc.*, trans. Trista Selous (Oxford: Blackwell, 1991). In French: *L'étude et le rouet* (Paris: Seuil, 1989). Quotations from this work will be identified parenthetically by page numbers.

2. Le Doeuff also finds instances of Sartre's obtuseness in *Existentialism and Humanism*, where Sartre declares: "Every purpose, even that of a Chinese, an Indian or a Negro, can be under-

stood by a European"; and "There is always some way of understanding an idiot, a child, a primitive man or a foreigner if one has
sufficient information." Le Doeuff's comment: "If you are not
laughing, I am wasting my time" (74).

3. Michèle Le Doeuff, *The Philosophical Imaginary* (Stanford: Stanford Univ. Press, 1989), 108–09.

4. Ibid., 109.

5. Ibid. The excerpts quoted by Le Doeuff are to be found in
the following works: Rousseau, *Emile*; Hegel, *Philosophy of Right*;
Comte, *Système de politique positive*, vol 2.

6. Antonio R. Damasio, *Descartes' Error: Emotion, Reason,
and the Human Brain* (New York: G. P. Putnam's Sons, 1994), 225.

7. Ibid., 89 and 213.

8. Ibid., xvi.

9. Ibid., 185.

10. Ibid., 181.

11. Ibid., 200.

12. Ibid., 262.

13. Ibid., 172.

14. Ibid., 260.

4. THE DIALECTIC OF REASON

1. Mitchell Dean, *Critical and Effective Histories: Foucault's
Methods and Historical Sociology* (New York: Routledge, 1994), 99.

2. Michel Foucault, "What Is Critique?" in *What Is Enlightenment: Eighteenth-century Answers and Twentieth-Century questions*,
ed. James Schmidt (Berkeley: Univ. of California Press, 1996), 391.

3. Ibid., 389.

4. Vincent Descombes, *The Barometer of Modern Reason:
On the Philosophies of Current Events*, trans. Stephen Adam
Schwartz (Oxford: Oxford Univ. Press, 1993), 44.

5. Ibid., 67–68.

6. Foucault, "What Is Critique?" 388.

7. Ibid.

8. Ibid., 389.

9. David Held, *Critical Theory* (Berkeley and Los Angeles:
Univ. of California Press, 1980), 229.

10. Ibid., 177.

11. Theodor W. Adorno, *Negative Dialectics* (New York:
Seabury, 1973), 406.

12. Herbert Marcuse, *Reason and Revolution* (Boston: Beacon Press, 1960), 49.

13. Theodor W. Adorno and Max Horkheimer, *Dialectic of Enlightenment* (New York: Herder & Herder, 1972), 15. Subsequent references will be indicated parenthetically in the text.

14. Foucault, "What Is Critique?" 389.

15. Dean, *Critical and Effective Histories*, 115.

16. David Couzens Hoy, "Foucault and Critical Theory," in *The Later Foucault* (forthcoming, to be published by Sage Press).

17. Descombes, *The Barometer of Modern Reason*, 144.

18. Hoy, "Foucault and Critical Theory."

19. Patrick Madigan, *The Modern Project to Rigor: Descartes to Nietzsche* (Lanham, Md.: Univ. Press of America, 1986), 54–55.

20. Held, *Critical Theory*, 396.

21. Dean, *Critical and Effective Histories*, 116.

22. Foucault, "What Is Critique?" 386.

23. Ibid., 387.

24. Ibid., 398.

25. Foucault, "The Art of Telling the Truth," in *Michel Foucault: Politics, Philosophy, Culture. Interviews and Other Writings, 1977–1984*, ed. Lawrence D. Kritzman, trans. Alan Sheridan et al. (New York: Routledge, 1988), 94–95.

26. Ibid., 392.

27. Ibid., 385–86.

28. Foucault, "What Is Critique?" 394.

29. Foucault, "The Art of Telling the Truth," 390 and 391.

30. Foucault, "Politics and Reason," in *Politics, Philosophy and Culture*, 83.

31. Dean, *Critical and Effective Histories*, 118.

32. Madigan, *The Modern Project to Rigor*, 181.

33. Michel Foucault, "Space, Knowledge, Power," in *The Foucault Reader*, ed. Paul Rabinow (New York: Pantheon, 1984), 249.

5. FOUCAULT'S CRITIQUE OF THE ENLIGHTENMENT

1. Hans-Georg Gadamer, *Truth and Method*, 262.

2. Michel Foucault, "What Is Enlightenment?" in *The Foucault Reader*, 45.

3. Ibid., 45–46.

4. Ibid., 42–43.

5. Michel Foucault, "Une histoire restée muette," *La Quinzaine littéraire* 8 (1–15 July 1966). *Dits et écrits* I (Paris: Gallimard, 1994): 547–48.

6. Foucault, "What Is Enlightenment?" 46.

7. Michael Mahon, *Foucault's Nietzschean Genealogy: Truth, Power, and the Subject* (Albany: SUNY Press, 1992), 126.

8. Michel Foucault, *The Archaeology of Knowledge*, trans. A. M. Sheridan Smith (New York: Pantheon, 1972), 36–37.

9. Foucault, "What Is Enlightenment?" 50.

10. Michel Foucault, *Remarks on Marx: Conversation with Duccio Trombadori*, trans. R. James Goldstein and James Cascaito (New York: Semiotext(e), 1991), 117–18. Translation modified.

11. Foucault, *The Archaeology of Knowledge*, 22.

12. Michel Foucault, "The Discourse on Language," trans. R. Swyer, in *The Archaeology of Knowledge*, 775.

13. Michel Foucault, "Politics and the Study of Discourse in *The Foucault Effect: Studies in Governmentality. With Two Lectures and an Interview with Michel Foucault*, ed. Graham Burchell, Colin Gordon, and Peter Miller, (Chicago: The Univ. of Chicago Press, 1991), 63.

14. Ibid., 61.

15. Ibid., 72.

16. Paul Veyne, *Comment on écrit l'histoire, suivi de Foucault révolutionne l'histoire* (Paris: Seuil, 1972), 215.

17. Michel Foucault, "Nietzsche, Freud, Marx," in *Dits et écrits* I, 564–65.

18. Foucault, "Politics and the Study of Discourse," 64.

19. Michel Foucault, "Le discours ne doit pas être pris comme . . ." in *Dits et écrits* III, 123.

20. Foucault, "Politics and the Study of Discourse," 63.

21. Michel Foucault, "Questions of Method," in *The Foucault Effect*, 85.

22. Foucault, "Le discours ne doit pas . . . ," 123–24.

23. Foucault, "What Is Enlightenment?" 47–48. Translation modified to include a missing line.

24. Ibid., 48.

25. Foucault, "Politics and the Study of Discourse," 65.

26. Foucault, "Nietzsche, Freud, Marx," 572.

27. Ibid., 573.

28. Ibid., 572.

29. Ibid., 571.

30. Roger Chartier, "The Chimera of the Origin: Archaeology, Cultural History, and the French Revolution, in *Foucault and the Writing of History*, ed. Jan Goldstein (Oxford: Blackwell, 1994), 184.

31. Ibid., 185.

32. Ibid., 180.

33. Ibid., 176.

34. Foucault, *The Archaeology of Knowledge*, 61.

35. Ibid.

36. Ibid., 146.

37. Chartier, "The Chimera of the Origin," 171.

38. Michel Foucault, "La philosophie analytique de la politique," in *Dits et écrits* vol. 3, 550.

39. Ibid.

40. Foucault, "Politics and the Study of Discourse," 56.

41. Ibid., 62.

42. Foucault, "What Is Enlightenment?" 50.

43. Ibid., 49.

44. Ibid., 46.

45. Ibid., 47.

46. Michel Foucault, "La vie: l'expérience et la science," in *Dits et écrits* IV, 768. The first version of this passage, published in 1978, reflected a more negative outlook on the Enlightenment's legacy: "Two centuries later, the Enlightenment returns: not as a way for the West to become aware of its present-day possibilities and of the freedoms to which it can have access, but as a way of questioning it about its limits and about the powers it has abused" (*Dits et écrits* III, 433).

6. REASON IN THE AGE OF ATROCITY

1. Stephen F. Cohen, "The Afterlife of Nikolai Bukharin," in Anna Larina, *This I Cannot Forget: The Memoirs of Nikolai Bukharin's Widow*, trans. Gary Kern (New York: W. W. Norton & Co., 1993), 4.

2. Carolyn Forché, (ed.), "Introduction," *Against Forgetting: Twentieth-Century Poetry of Witness* (New York: W. W. Norton & Co., 1993), 29.

3. *Into the Whirlwind*, trans. by Paul Stevenson and Max Hayward (New York: Harcourt, Brace & World, 1967), and *Within the Whirlwind*, trans. by Ian Boland (New York: Harcourt, Brace & Jovanovich, 1981). References to these works will be noted parenthetically by volume and page number.

4. Adam Michnik, *Letters from Prison and Other Essays* (Berkeley: Univ. of California Press, 1984), 201.

5. Joseph Berger, *Le naufrage d'une génération* (Paris: Denoël, 1974), 53. Quoted by Slavoj Zizek, "Essai sur l'"herméneutique' stalinienne," in *Généalogie de la politique 2: Actes du Colloque de Milan, 1977*, ed. Armando Verdiglione (Paris: UGE, 1978), 101.

6. Ibid., 98.

7. Ibid., 102.

8. Ibid.

9. Robert Conquest, *Stalin and the Kirov Murder* (Oxford: Oxford Univ. Press, 1989), 3 and 87–88. Although Stalin was thought, for a long time, to have instigated the murder, this hypothesis now seems doubtful in light of Alla Kirilina's research. See her book, *L'Assasinat de Kirov: Destin d'un stalinien, 1888–1934* (Paris: Seuil, 1995). Stalin's direct involvement in the purges that followed is a well established fact, however. In the period 1937–1938 he signed personally some 40,000 execution orders.

10. Adam Hochschild, *The Unquiet Ghost: Russia Remembers Stalin* (New York: Viking, 1994), 223.

11. Ibid., 77. In this regard, the functioning of the NKVD not only reflected that of the general economy and its goals of five-year plans but its reliance on a purely imaginary reality provided a model for a similar strategy in the economic domain; by the end of the Soviet regime, the statistics concerning economic productivity were being systematically inflated with nonexistent factory outputs and harvests from imaginary collective farms.

12. Ibid., p. 23.

13. Vasya is today Vassily Aksyonov, one of today's better known Russian novelists. His latest works appearing in English are *Generations of Winter*, trans. John Glad and Christopher Morris (New York: Random House, 1994), a novel evoking life in Russia during the period of Stalin's purges, and its sequel, *The Winter's Hero*, trans. John Glad (New York: Random House, 1996), covering years between the end of World War II and the death of Stalin.

14. Hannah Arendt, *The Human Condition* (Chicago: The Univ. of Chicago Press, 1958), 228.

15. Alain Finkielkraut, *La mémoire vaine: Du crime contre l'humanité* (Paris: Gallimard, 1989), 98.

16. Hannah Arendt, *Le système totalitaire* (Paris: Seuil, 1972), 216–17.

17. Finkielkraut, *La mémoire vaine*, 100.

18. Ibid.

19. Quoted in Hochschild, *The Unquiet Ghost*, 138.

20. Jeremy Varon, "The Dreadful Concatenation: Modernity and Massacre in Todorov, Adorno and Horkheimer," *New German Critique* 59 (1993): 175–76.

21. Geneviève Even-Granboulan, *Action et Raison* (Paris: Méridiens-Klincksieck, 1986), 278.

22. The Proceedings of the conference have been published as *History, Society and the Individual: Theme of the 18th World Congress of Philosophy (Brighton, August 1988)*, "Social Sciences Today" Editorial Board (Moscow: USSR Academy of Sciences, Institute of Philosophy, 1988). Page numbers will be indicated in parentheses.

7. ETHNIC IDENTITY IN A POST-STALINIST AGE

1. *The New York Times*, June 17, 1990, Section H, 5.

2. Other more subtle policies were also implemented: young people of Baltic origin were not allowed to pursue higher education in the Baltics but had to go to faraway places in other parts of the Soviet Union; young men were also sent far away for their military training. They often found themselves in units where the active harassment and persecution of Baltic nationals was encouraged by the officers in charge. There were a number of cases where the recruit died under mysterious circumstances.

3. Anita Rozkalne, "Par latviesu prozu," *Literatura un Maksla*, 29 April, 1994, 6.

4. Clare Cavanagh, "Rereading the Poet's Ending: Mandelstam, Chaplin, and Stalin," *PMLA* 109 (1994): 72.

5. Maris Caklais, "Tiksimies tekstos!" *Literatura un Maksla*, 29 April 1994, 6.

6. Forché, *Against Forgetting*, p. 31.

7. See Stéphane Courtois et al., *Le livre noir du communisme: Crimes, terreur, répression* (Paris: Robert Laffont, 1997), 263. See also the special report of the House Select Committee on Communist Aggression, *Communist Takeover and Occupation of Latvia*, House Report No. 2684, Part 1, 83d Cong., 2d sess., 30 December, 1954, 24–25. In his introduction to *Via Dolorosa*, Janis Stradins cites a much more conservative estimate of 120 to 160 thousand.

8. *These Names Accuse: Nominal List of Latvians Deported to Soviet Russia in 1940–41*, Stockholm: The Latvian National Foundation, 1951.

9. The notable ones are: Rasma Aizupe, *Sespadsmit gadi Sibirija* [Sixteen Years in Siberia], Toronto: Alta, 1974; Janis Simsons, *Vorkutas gustekna stasts* [The Story of a Prisoner in Vorkuta], Lincoln, Neb.: Vaidava, 1965; Lilija Zarina, *Sarkana migla* [The Red Fog], Toronto: Daugavas Vanags, 1968. Also to be mentioned is the wrenching account by a girl who was fourteen when she was deported with her family: Rutina U., *Vel ta gribejas dzivot* [I Wanted So to Live], New York: Gramatu Draugs, 1977. The diary was also published as *Dear God, I Wanted to Live* in an English translation that is, unfortunately, inept. The work has also been translated in German. Of the authors included in *Via dolorosa*, several have appeared in separate publications. The poems of Janis Medenis are assembled in the cycles "Putnu cels" [The Path of Birds], "Norilskas vainags" [The Crown of Norilsk], and "Ziemelu elegijas" [Northern Elegies] in vol. 4 of his complete works, *Raksti IV*, Grand Rapids: Aiviekste, 1988. Melanija Vanaga has published the book-length narrative *Velupes krasta, 1941–1957* [On the Shores of the River of Departed Souls], Riga: Liesma, 1991. The poems in which Bronislava Martuzeva records her Siberian experience have been collected in her *Celu Krusti* [Road Crosses], Riga: Liesma, 1990.

10. *Literatura un Maksla*, 25 March 1989, 9.

11. *Literatura un Maksla*, 21 January 1989, 13.

12. Latvian folk songs have been preserved thanks to a vast project of collecting and writing down this oral tradition that was undertaken in the last decades of the nineteenth century. The assembling of the *dainas* was mainly the work of one man—Krisjanis Barons. Between 1894 and 1915, he published more than two hundred thousand *dainas*, a total that included some thirty-five thousand basic or standard versions and one hundred and eighty thousand variants.

13. Marija Gimbutas, *The Goddesses and Gods of Old Europe* (Berkeley: The Univ. of California Press, 1982), 9.

14. Forché, *Against Forgetting*, 43.

15. Ibid.

16. Ernesto Laclau, "Universalism, Particularism, and the Question of Identity," in *The Identity in Question*, ed. and introd. by John Rajchman (New York and London: Routledge, 1995), 94. Quotations from this essay will be identified parenthetically in the text.

17. Forché, *Against Forgetting*, 37.

18. Gregory Bruce Smith, *Nietzsche, Heidegger, and the Transition to Postmodernity* (Chicago: The Univ. of Chicago Press, 1996), 337.

19. François Dubet, *Sociologie de l'expérience*, 101.

EPILOGUE

1. Michel Foucault, "Nietzsche, Genealogy, History," in *Language, Counter-Memory, Practice*, ed. Donald F. Bouchard (Ithaca: Cornell Univ. Press, 1977), 153.

2. The best known statement to this effect is Francis Fukuyama's "End of History" thesis.

3. William Greider, *One World, Ready or Not: The Manic Logic of Global Capitalism* (New York: Simon & Schuster, 1997), 11.

4. Ibid., 137.

5. Ibid., 388.

6. Ibid., 381.

7. I have already developed some of these arguments earlier, in *Postmodernism and the Search for the Enlightenment*; see, for example, Chapter 7, "The Politics of a Postmodern Critique."

8. Greider, *One World*, 383.

9. Lester Thurow, "Companies Merge; Families Break Up," *The New York Times Week in Review*, 3 September 1995, 11.

10. Katherine Paterson, "Family Values: Advice on how to raise ethical children from William J. Bennett and a prominent rabbi," *The New York Times Book Review*, 3 September 1995, 32.

11. Greider, *One World*, 440.

12. Georgia Warnke, 208.

13. Régis Debray, 244.

14. Jean-Luc Nancy, *L'oubli de la philosophie*, 105.

15. ———— , *Etre singulier pluriel*, 67–68.

16. Stjepan G. Mestrovic, *The Barbarian Temperament: Towards a Postmodern Critical Theory* (Oxford: Routledge, 1993), 76.

17. Michèle Le Doeuff, *The Philosophical Imaginary*, 117.

18. Ibid., 118.

19. Nancy, *Etre singulier pluriel*, 112.

20. Michel Foucault, "What Is Enlightenment?" 46–47.

21. Friedrich Nietzsche, *Thus Spoke Zarathustra*, trans. with a preface by Walter Kaufmann (New York: Penguin, 1978), 76.

22. Gerda Lerner, *Why History Matters: Life and Thought* (New York and Oxford: Oxford Univ. Press, 1997), 53.

23. John Deely, *New Beginnings: Early Modern Philosophy and Postmodern Thought* (Toronto: The Univ. of Toronto Press, 1994), 17.

24. Ibid., 27.

25. Ibid., 3. Deely is particularly interested in bringing to light the work of John Poinsot (1589–1644), which provides an entry to "twelve-hundred years of the Latin Age, but brings into particular focus its last three centuries as seen from Iberia" (31). Poinsot's writings, Deely shows, prefigure in a remarkable way the work of Charles S. Peirce.

26. Achille Mbembe, "Prosaics of Servitude and Authoritarian Civilities," *Public Culture* 5 (1992): 142.

27. Biodun Jeyifo, "Oguntoyinbo: Modernity and the 'Rediscovery' Phase of Postcolonial Literature," *Yearbook of Comparative and General Literature* 43 (1995): 99.

28. Ibid., 106. Jeyifo proposes the writings of Wole Soyinka as particularly successful examples of such a strategy.

29. Ibid.

30. Nana Wilson-Tagoe, "Post-Colonial Literary Theory and the Theorizing of African Literature," *Yearbook*, 111.

31. Alioune Diop, "Opening Address," *Yearbook*, 10. Diop is the founder of the publishing house "Présence africaine" and its journal.

32. Eileen Julien, "African Literatures in Comparative Perspective," *Yearbook*, 19.

33. Wilson-Tagoe, "Post-Colonial Literary Theory," 115.

34. Mbembe, "Prosaics of Servitude," 145.

Index